# Managing People

Vivien Whitaker, MSc OD, ~~describes her~~ change': she works with people to assist them to make their organizations more effective. Her consultancy has included projects on problem-solving, strategic planning, management of change, team development and action learning-based management development, and she has worked with a wide variety of private and public sector organizations. Vivien also writes workbooks focused on solving performance problems and is currently writing a book on self-development entitled *Letting Go*.

Bob Garratt is a company director, consultant and academic. He is Chairman of Media Projects International in London and of Organization Development Limited in Hong Kong. He consults in director development and the development of strategic thinking in Europe, Asia, Australia, New Zealand, and the USA. He is Visiting Fellow at the Management School of Imperial College, London University, an associate of the Judge Institute of Management, Cambridge University and immediate past chairman of the Association for Management Education and Development.

Other titles in the Successful Manager series:

Titles in the Successful Strategist series

VIVIEN WHITAKER

# Managing People

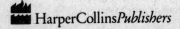
HarperCollins*Publishers*

for David

HarperCollins*Publishers*
77–85 Fulham Palace Road,
Hammersmith, London W6 8JB

A Paperback Original 1994
9 8 7 6 5 4 3 2 1

Copyright © Vivien Whitaker 1994

The Author asserts the moral right to
be identified as the author of this work

A catalogue record for this book
is available from the British Library

ISBN 0 00 637933 8

Set in Palatino and Helvetica

Printed in Great Britain by
HarperCollinsManufacturing Glasgow

# Contents

# Preface

For twelve years, I have been working with people to help them make their organizations more effective. Much of my time with managers is spent in problem-solving, team development and management development programmes.

This has involved my doing a post round (with a postwoman called Pat) at 5 a.m. on a stormy January morning, whilst working with Royal Mail. It has taken me on to a gas platform in Scotland, working with BP Exploration. I have worked with volunteer managers in Nipa huts in the Philippines and shared 'the best of western management ideas' with trainee managers in newly-liberated Czechoslovakia.

I describe myself as a 'catalyst for change'. It is my job to enable other people to improve their effectiveness. However, unlike a catalyst, I do not remain inert over time. I have grown to love risk-taking, and continue to learn and improve my effectiveness day by day.

I have interpreted the experiences of practising managers, related these to relevant theories and created some new models for managing people. My father says that a lot of my work is applied Lancastrian common sense. I respond with a quote from Rosabeth Moss Kanter, of Harvard Business School: 'It may be very sensible, but in my experience it is not very common.'

I hope you enjoy reading this book and find that the ideas make sense for you in your work.

# Acknowledgements

**Special thanks to**
David Meggison, Jane Coddington, Kath Attenborough, Bob
Garratt, Lucinda McNeile, Annabel Marsh, Juliet Van Oss,
John Perkins, Maggie Stubbs, Cheryle Berry, Frank Lord,
Liz Cross, Philip Lewer, Edward Megginson and Katherine
Megginson.

**Thanks for their help to**
Geoff Atkinson, Peter Beamiss, Andrew Burns, John Carlisle,
Brian Coddington, Peter Collett, Keith Crawshaw, Tony Crisp,
Jackie Delaney, Neil Fenton, Ian Flemming, Tim Griggs, Helen
Hanslip, Nigel Harrison, Phil Hodgson, Helen Holmes,
Melanie Hollinshead, John Hughes, Janet James, Nicky Keogh,
Jeanette Kozimor, Suzanne Lecke, John Lomas, John Lowther,
Bill McDermott, Mike Pedler, Cath Morris, Raymond Morris,
Roy Morris, Wendy Parkin, Grant Peggie, Vicky Philsoph,
Jenny Pupius, Mike Pupius, Tom Richardson, Steve Rick,
John Sewell, Jan Shutt, Annie Southers, Bryan Smith, Ken
Smith, John Stannard, Terry Tallis, Roger Taylor, David Tow,
Peter Townsend, Clare Ward, Richard Wells, David Whitaker,
Gladys Whitaker, John Youatt and all the people I have worked
with in the past, and my current clients. Thank you all for
sharing your ideas, your learning and your experiences.

# Introduction

There are many myths which surround the way we manage people:

Good managers are born and not made

People only come to work to earn money

I can't change my management style because that would change my personality

You need to treat people like machines to get results

I am a 'bad people manager' as I wasn't able to handle a difficult older member of staff when I first became a manager

Professionals don't need to be managed

There is only one right way to manage people

Some of these prejudices have developed as a result of past attitudes to work and management. Often they will remain in organizations long after the attitudes themselves have fallen into misuse. These myths can act as a powerful influence preventing us from exploring and challenging the way we manage people. These myths, like all myths, are not true.

This book sets out to dispel these myths and offers new and better approaches to managing people. It

- provides a blueprint to help managers change their style of management
- is designed not just for the new manager or the young manager, but also for the manager who believes he/she cannot change

- looks at the cost of not changing the way we manage people
- introduces new Positive Assumptions which help us to manage people effectively
- describes Seven Keys to Success in managing people
- helps managers to identify and build on their strengths in managing people and further develop their skills
- recognizes that learning to manage people is a continuous process.

Janet James, a senior teacher of nursing, comments:

*The ideas in this book seem to go straight to the core of changing behaviours and attitudes rather than theorizing too much around the issues.*

Dr Cheryle Berry, head teacher of High Storrs School in Sheffield, was delighted with both the Assumptions and the Seven Keys to Success.

*It's the first time I have seen the approach that my staff and I take written up in such an accessible way. It works tremendously well; it's fun and gives us great job satisfaction.*

Other managers have used the ideas in this book to transform the way they see their role. One manager remarked:

*I felt disempowered within a bureaucracy and I believed that what I did made no difference. I was encouraged to challenge this thinking and adopt new ideas and approaches and I now feel both more effective and happier in my work.*

Managers achieve results through other people. Improving your skills in managing people can, therefore, help you achieve better results. John Harvey-Jones estimates that employees typically use forty per cent of their potential at work. On this basis there is a lot of scope for improvement, at little extra cost.

The Japanese have two words for optimism. The first, when translated, fits with our own 'bright, hopeful view of things' interpretation. The second means having enough challenges in life to keep you busy. This book is designed to help you to be optimistic, in both senses of the word.

# The Need to Manage People

Managers achieve results through other people. Management gurus are convinced that it is vital that we rethink the way we manage our relationships with our staff to enable us to enhance effectiveness and maximize performance, productivity and profits within our organizations.

Charles Handy[1] observes that:

*We live in an age of unreason when we can no longer assume that what worked well once will work well again, when most assumptions can be legitimately challenged.*

Brian Dumaine,[2] in his article 'The New Non-Manager Managers', confirms that the traditional role of the manager is under threat and describes a new breed of manager:

*Call them sponsors, facilitators − anything but the M-word. They're helping their companies and advancing their careers by turning old management practices upside down.*

Rosemary Stewart,[3] author of *Managing Today and Tomorrow*, has also noted this pattern and believes such changes will make management more rewarding.

*The many changes in managers' jobs mean that managers must broaden their knowledge, learn new skills and become more adept in their ability to influence others; they are under more pressure to make effective and efficient use of resources.*

## Threat to Traditional Managers

Traditionally, managers focused primarily on administration

and distribution of information. This is no longer the case. There is a growing pressure for managers to recognize the need to transform their approach to management. The threat to traditional American managers is real. Brian Dumaine commented in February 1993:

> *It's still open season on the American middle manager, and big guns begin to bag their daily limit without difficulty. Hardly a day passes without some formerly blue chip outfit like GM, IBM or Sears dispatching another couple of thousand or so to the corporate afterlife. The American Management Association reports that while middle managers are only five per cent of the workforce at the 836 companies it surveyed, they account for a plump twenty-two per cent of last year's layoffs.*

The trend is well documented in the US but is also gathering strength in Britain and Europe. The Institute of Management in Britain carried out a survey of more than 800 of its members' careers over the past thirteen years.[4] It found that twenty-nine per cent changed jobs in 1992 and that enforced moves – particularly redundancies and changes resulting from company restructuring – were the main reasons for these moves.

## Reacting to This Threat

Managers have a choice about the way they react to this threat. As professionals in a changing environment they are like Charles Handy's frogs in water. The water is heating up around them, in the form of changes created by market pressures, new legislation, the introduction of information technology or different working practices (for example, single union agreements), and/or from operating within a trans-national or global arena, rather than a national one.

If managers can acknowledge what is happening and jump out they can change their approach and survive. If they don't recognize that the temperature is rising or if they resist change, they will be boiled to death; they will not survive in their role as a manager.

This book is designed to help managers recognize that the water is heating up. It encourages you to look upon this situation as an opportunity to jump out of the water and begin to learn new skills and approaches which will equip you, as a manager, to survive successfully in today's fast-changing environment.

## Fear of Change

Some managers doubt that they can change, even when they know that the way they are behaving is hindering their aims. They fear they are 'too old' or 'too cautious' or 'too set in their ways'. Henry Ford once commented: 'If you believe you can or if you believe you can't; you're right.' If you think you can change, you will; if you stick with the belief you can't, you won't.

Behavioural scientists tell us that we can change our

behaviour within a month if we practise the new behaviour consistently every day for thirty days.

## Choosing to Change from Traditional Management

I would like to describe the way two 'traditional' managers, one in a large PLC, the other an owner-manager, chose to change the way they managed people.

### *John Perkins, Chief Engineer at British Airways*

John has worked in engineering for more than thirty years. His nickname used to be the 'Rambo Manager of Fortress Engineering'. He commented publicly in 1992: 'I don't mind admitting I was a "Rambo-style" manager – I have changed my own style because I have seen that it is just not the most successful way.'[5]

His staff often went on strike in protest about their treatment and conditions. During a particularly long and bitter strike John recognized that something or someone had to change. When the strike was resolved he went to Harvard for a three-month study of alternative methods of managing. He returned with an in-depth understanding of people management and started progressively to implement these ideas. He describes his new management style in chapter 6. Chapter 2 provides details of how the implementation of John's ideas saved British Airways twenty-five million pounds.

I asked John what he thought the benefits of changing his management style were. He smiled and said: 'I've had more professional success in the last two and a half years than I had in the previous ten years. I have less pain, no tears . . . and I smile more often.'

### *Nicky Keogh, of Keyo Agricultural Services*

Nicky decided that he wanted to change the way he managed his business when he was in his mid-thirties.

5

Keyo Agricultural Services was established twenty-five years ago to serve a specialized niche in the poultry supply industry. Nicky took over the family business and began managing the business in the same patriarchal way as his brother and father had done. However he soon found that he was getting bored, and decided he needed to broaden his thinking. Keyo had a good management team but staff turnover was high as they too were bored; they didn't feel they were being delegated enough responsibility.

Nicky chose to increase his skills by enrolling on an MBA. As his studies progressed he became aware that his patriarchal management style was hindering the success of his organization, rather than helping it. Nicky acknowledged that there were a number of potential benefits that could arise from changing his management style yet he wasn't sure that he could make the necessary changes.

He decided to make a determined effort to change over a period of one month. Each morning he got up half an hour earlier to 'talk himself into his new style'. He identified what he was going to do differently each day and how he could progressively surprise his staff with his new 'nice and open' management style.

Many things changed at Keyo Agricultural Services. Nicky initiated sessions for the management team focusing on self-development and organization development, he delegated more responsibility and accountability to the team, funded development plans for team members (irrespective of whether they were work-related) and pioneered opportunities for diversification.

One of his management team said to him some months afterwards: 'I used to hate my job and harboured secret plans to leave. I now get up early every morning with a spring in my stride. It's become exciting and challenging to work in this firm.' Nicky's family were also delighted by the changes and declared that he had become much easier to live with too.

The test of this new style came when Keyo's biggest customer suddenly stopped using their services. They lost half their business at a stroke. Before these changes Nicky would have tried to deal with the crisis alone. Instead he worked with his management team, diversified services to Keyo's other major customer and reshaped the company. Nicky admits that if this crisis had occurred before he initiated the changes in management style, Keyo would probably have ceased trading.

# 2

# The Cost of Not Managing People

One of the first things I do when I start work on a new project with an organization is help them to calculate the cost of not undertaking that project. It isn't possible to work it out exactly but we can create approximate figures to act as a rough and ready estimate. Calculating this cost often proves to be a powerful motivator to change the way things get done.

When I was working with someone from an open learning institution we found that an irritant for him, as an editor, was the inaccurate keying-in of editors' marks by typists. We calculated that this was costing his organization several thousand pounds a year. The solution that we created together – written aides-mémoire on the typists' word processors and on the wall in their office – cost very little.

When I worked with British Rail Safety Executive on a project on trackside safety, we were calculating success in terms of how many accidents could be prevented and how many lives could be saved as a result of a new initiative.

Could you apply this idea to your part of your own organization? What is the cost of your *not* providing an effective service of management to your staff and colleagues?

Think of your staff and colleagues as internal customers who are receiving a service from you. Now let's assess whether they are receiving the same or a similar service to that of the external customers of your organization.

Working with external customers often involves:

1. Listening and communicating with them, as fully as possible

2. Ensuring they are making the best use of the equipment/service provided
3. Responding to their complaints
4. Involving them in improving service
5. Providing thanks, when appropriate
6. Showing respect (and not losing your temper)
7. Being available to respond to their needs.

Now consider the potential costs you could incur if these issues were not fully taken into account when working with staff and colleagues. Using your part of your organization – your team or your department – carry out the following analysis.

## The Hidden Costs Involved in Not Managing People Effectively

This analysis takes the seven aspects of external customer service and helps you to apply them to your internal customers. It starts from the principle that you and your colleagues are working to provide a good service of management to your internal customers and it is designed to highlight areas where you could further improve this service.

You can either undertake this exercise on your own, or with a colleague, or with your team. It is sometimes easier to create these approximate assessments after discussing them with another person.

Calculate the approximate costs *per year for each item*, or if it is easier, *each week*, and then multiply the amount by fifty-two.

|  | **Weekly** | **Yearly** |
|---|---|---|
| 1. Cost of duplication of effort, due to inadequate communication | £ | £ |
| 2. Costs of not using the equipment you have available to best advantage | £ | £ |

3. Cost of time spent complaining to   £        £
   colleagues
   - by me
   - by my staff

4. Cost of not seeking ideas for        £        £
   improvement from the person who
   does the job

5. Cost of loss of staff motivation      £        £
   through not receiving appropriate
   thanks from you, or others

6. Cost of loss of long-term co-operation  £       £
   through inappropriate loss of temper

7. Cost of sickness/absenteeism and staff  £       £
   turnover

   Our current sickness/absenteeism rate
   is   % pa
   This costs us:
   - sick pay                     £
   - additional personnel to cover      £
   - disruption to other staff        £

   Our current staff turnover is   % pa
   This costs us:
   advertising                 £
   recruitment interviews       £
   hours lost interviewing      £
   induction into new job      £
   effect on other staff/production   £

   Other costs – list any additional costs   £

   Total Cost of Not Managing People Effectively  £

## Using Your Calculations to Create Change

This analysis will

- highlight significant costs
- indicate where change is needed
- focus on issues which you, as a manager, can influence.

Frequently, when managers realize how much their present way of working is costing them, they become motivated to improve the way things get done in their part of the organization.

Think about how you can use the information you have collected:

- Would it be useful in arguing for more, or different, resources for your section?
- Could it help you create a case for changing systems and procedures?
- Has it provided you with feedback which means you need to plan to do things differently in the future?

It is useful to follow this learning cycle when thinking of doing things differently.

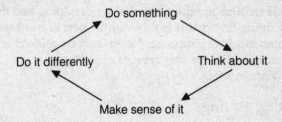

Let us follow this cycle to analyse a situation where someone lost their temper inappropriately with colleagues.

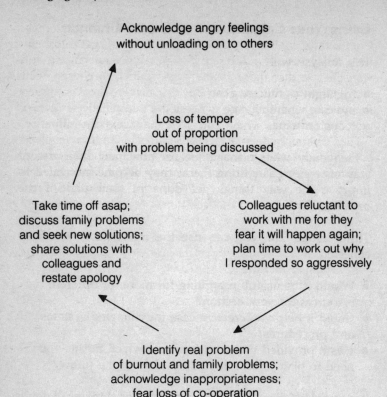

Acknowledge angry feelings
without unloading on to others

Loss of temper
out of proportion
with problem being discussed

Take time off asap;
discuss family problems
and seek new solutions;
share solutions with
colleagues and
restate apology

Colleagues reluctant to
work with me for they
fear it will happen again;
plan time to work out why
I responded so aggressively

Identify real problem
of burnout and family problems;
acknowledge inappropriateness;
fear loss of co-operation

Sometimes we can be so busy with urgent demands that we don't create time to reflect on what we are doing and the way we are doing it. Yet this is an essential part of our long-term development. Many successful managers set aside at least ten minutes each day for this type of reflection.

## Creating Savings

Involving your team or colleagues in reflection and planning changes may also save you money and improve effectiveness. Royal Mail in Sheffield decided to involve their staff in the redesign and refurbishment of one part of the sorting office. Comfortable chairs were essential for the staff, yet the chairs they chose were of a different design, a different colour, and were cheaper than those the manager would have chosen. Staff suggestions for changing the way things were done improved the workflow. Output rose as a result of this initiative and error rate was reduced.

The Community Mental Health Services in Bradford involved both staff and users in their plans for improving their service. This had a significant impact on users – the occupancy levels at day centres increased by 135 per cent. It also had a real impact on staff sickness and staff turnover, both of which were reduced by seventy per cent in the subsequent year.

John Perkins, the chief engineer at British Airways, was asked to cut £8.25 million from his budget as a result of losses in revenue at the time of the Gulf War in 1990. He chose to involve both staff and unions in identifying where savings could be made. He sought out members of staff from all the workshops who were interested in working on the problem. These people worked together and created the SMART initiative.

Saving
Maintenance and
Aircraft
Resources
Together

The objectives of the SMART initiative were

To save £10 million in the 91/92 budget
To be more efficient and productive
To protect job security
To reduce subcontracting
To increase third-party work
To be achieved by working together

The SMART initiative achieved savings of £25 *Million*.

## Motivation For Free

Rosabeth Moss Kanter wrote a short, lighthearted article about the importance of saying 'thank you'. She received many letters in response. A chemical company asked her to go and give a seminar on 'how to say thank you'. She rang them and asked why they needed a seminar. Their response was that to say 'thank you' in their organization would be showing too much emotion.

Receiving appropriate thanks is ranked as one of the highest rated motivators of staff. Saying 'thank you' doesn't cost anything, takes less than a minute and makes someone work more enthusiastically.

# Learning a Different Approach

When we are considering doing things differently it is sometimes difficult to know where to start. How do we identify new ideas and different ways of doing things? During busy working days it often feels simpler and more comfortable to do what we've always done. However, if you do what you've always done, you tend to get the same results as before; and that's not always appropriate.

In this chapter we look initially at some ideas which can help you to change the way you approach issues relating to managing people. We then look at seven problems which illustrate a range of common dilemmas relating to managing people and present a range of different ways of responding to those dilemmas.

## Customer focus

The first idea we are going to explore is that of customer focus or customer orientation. We need to redesign the systems and structures within our organizations so that they help, rather than hinder, the people who use our services or products. Traditional organizations, working as hierarchies, need to have their customer focus turned upside down.

## *Traditional organization*

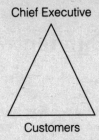

The new customer focus turns the triangle on its head and puts the customer at the top; so everyone, including the chief executive, is serving someone who is serving the customer.

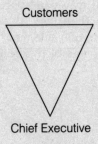

The chain of staff, who are serving other staff who are serving the customer, is referred to as an *internal customer chain*. Staff in these chains are both *internal customers* – they receive a service from someone, and *internal suppliers* – they provide a service to someone.

## Providing a service of management

Management of people described in these terms is about being a *supplier of management* — to your staff, and a *customer of your line manager* — receiving a service of management from them.

A manager's internal customer-supplier chains may look like this in an organization with a traditional hierarchy:

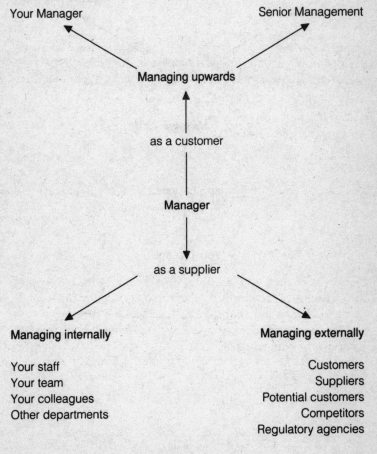

Your Manager  Senior Management

Managing upwards

as a customer

Manager

as a supplier

**Managing internally**  **Managing externally**

Your staff  Customers
Your team  Suppliers
Your colleagues  Potential customers
Other departments  Competitors
Regulatory agencies

A customer-focused organization will look like this:

**Managing internally**                    **Managing externally**

Your staff                                              Customers
Your team                                               Suppliers
Your colleagues                          Potential customers
Other departments                              Competitors
                                                    Regulatory agencies

as a supplier

Manager

as a customer

Your manager

Senior management

You will see that the process of providing a service of management to people is clearly mapped out. If this process is applied in practice it provides the opportunity for managers as suppliers of a service of management to ask a range of their internal customers:

> *Am I supplying you with a service of management which meets your needs as a customer of mine?*

> *If I am not meeting your needs, then let's discuss what I need to do differently.*

It also creates the opportunity for a manager as a customer to say legitimately to his/her line manager and senior managers either:

> *I am a satisfied customer of yours and I really appreciate the service of management you are providing.*

> *or*

> *I am a customer of yours and you are not providing me with the service of management I require. I would like to discuss this with you.*

## Exploring these ideas through resolving problems

The problems which follow describe common management dilemmas. They offer you the opportunity to consider each situation from the point of view of a manager who is providing a service of management to his/her staff. Each problem invites you to select the solution that you think is the most appropriate. Please indicate your choice by ticking a box.

## *Problem 1*

An Asian woman manager was talking to her line manager. 'Sometimes the other managers act as if I'm not there in meetings. Outside of meetings it can be worse. I agree deadlines with Mike and follow them up with a written note but he never does things on time. When I complain, he says that I'm nagging at him, like his wife. I find it so hard to make a stand as I was brought up not to talk back to men and to keep in my place.'

If you were her line manager would you recommend that she:

1. stop taking things so seriously ☐

2. enrol on an assertiveness course ☐

3. separate home from work, and confront her with the fact that she is 'playing victim' at work and needs to develop new strategies for dealing with difficult situations. ☐

## *Problem 2*

A team leader, relatively new to an organization, and his manager were discussing the team leader's poor performance. The new team leader had good references but had taken a lateral move for family reasons. Yet he was not getting even the basic management tasks right. Further discussions revealed that the team leader had done 'all of that' before, was not interested in it, and saw himself as being 'above' doing these basic tasks. He was, however, interested in a network marketing idea which he was developing with a friend (external to work) and was putting all his energies into that.

If you were the manager would you:

1. give the team leader a month to get his act together ☐

2. administer a formal verbal warning ☐

3. gain structured feedback from the team leader and his team about what was not working effectively. Involve the team leader in discussing this feedback and developing an action plan for change. ☐

## Problem 3

Staff at the head office of a government agency were organizing a European conference. They were discussing ways of getting continuous feedback throughout the conference. It was decided that someone should be found to go round during the breaks interviewing senior representatives from a variety of European countries to collect immediate responses. This feedback would be used to adapt the conference to the needs of the participants, if this proved necessary.

If you were the manager would you:

1. contact the marketing section and ask them to provide this service ☐

2. find an external consultant to provide this service ☐

3. use a clerical officer who had been very involved in organizing the conference (such duties are not in her job description and would normally be done by an officer of a higher grade). ☐

## Problem 4

A personnel officer for a local authority department has received a number of complaints about sexual harassment from the female staff of a manager in his twenties. She talks to the staff concerned and arranges to have a formal interview with the manager and the NALGO shop steward. During the formal interview the manager does not deny what has been happening but is shocked that his behaviour has been interpreted in this way. Both the manager and the shop steward agree that the allegations are proven and accept that the manager has been failing in his responsibilities. The personnel officer has now to decide what action should be taken.

If you were the personnel officer would you:

1. do nothing on the grounds that the manager has learned his lesson ☐

2. give the manager a formal warning to indicate to him, and other staff, that sexual harassment is something that the authority takes seriously ☐

3. focus on the manager's need for development and seek out a course which would help him gain greater understanding of the issues involved. ☐

## *Problem 5*

It is 10.30 a.m. on a Monday morning in a small manufacturing company. The managing director's secretary is apologizing to callers as her boss has not arrived yet. She turns to a colleague, who is also seeking the MD, and says, 'I hope he's not going to make me work late tonight. I've arranged to go to the pictures with Phil.' The colleague responds, 'The frustrating thing is that he knows that his time-keeping habits make it difficult for us. We all gave him feedback about it on a recent time management course.' They both agree to confront him with the problem when he arrives at work.

If you were the managing director would you:

1. do nothing. After all it's your company ☐

2. adjust your hours to those of the company ☐

3. schedule meetings for later in the day and negotiate overtime with your secretary, in advance. ☐

## *Problem 6*

A new managing director was helping a team of regional managers in a retail company to review the way they worked together. Their industry was a very competitive one and their behaviour within the team was competitive too. One member of the team had been with the company for twenty years and had a wealth of experience; another had been with a sister company which made higher profits; the third, a recent recruit to the company, was ambitious and had just been promoted. Each thought their own approach to managing their region was the right one. The new managing director talked about the philosophy of co-operation and teamwork. The company was losing market share and he was seeking new ways of motivating staff to reverse this trend.

If you were in the managing director's shoes would you:

1. set stiffer targets for each region and award performance-related benefits for the region which achieved the highest sales ☐

2. make the older manager redundant and bring in 'younger blood' ☐

3. bring in consultants to work with the regional managers: assisting in the redefinition of their roles, evaluating each regional manager's experience, and enabling them to work together towards achieving higher profits in all regions. ☐

## Problem 7

The manager of a physiotherapy department in a psychiatric hospital was involved in a discussion with the manager of the occupational therapy department. The subject of their discussion was a number of requests that had been received, from patients, for therapeutic massage. 'We've never done this before. Why should we do it now? We're not a private clinic,' said the occupational therapist. 'We are committed to being customer-oriented though, aren't we?' responded the physiotherapist, adding, 'Many of our patients live alone and may not be touched by anyone. It might aid their recovery.'

If you were these managers would you:

1. carry on providing the traditional services of each department ☐

2. develop a register of therapeutic masseurs who work in the hospital catchment area ☐

3. agree that the physiotherapist will create a 'pilot' therapeutic massage service for a period of three months and monitor the results. □

All these case studies highlight that there are a range of solutions to each problem. Each case study was based on a real situation and Option 3 was the solution chosen, in all cases, by the people involved.

## Did the solutions work?

Yes they did.

### *The results*

### *Case Study 1*

The confrontation and labelling as a 'victim' shocked the manager and motivated her to change her behaviour at work. She initially practised putting forward her point of view in discussion with individuals. When she had gained confidence she altered her behaviour in meetings. After a few months she realized she enjoyed coming to work more and was achieving better results.

### *Case Study 2*

The manager, the team leader and his team all completed a questionnaire about the team leader's performance (see chapter 7 for details of the questionnaire). The manager and the team leader assessed the results and drew up an action plan for change in which they both identified areas that needed to be improved. The action plan was reviewed during their subsequent supervision sessions and progress was identified and appreciated by all concerned.

## Case Study 3

The clerical officer was approached and agreed to do the interviewing, as long as she received coaching and support from a colleague. She carried out all the interviews and the feedback that she collected helped make the conference responsive and successful. When she was asked, 'How did it go?' she said, 'It was great. I'd love to do it again.'

## Case Study 4

The manager attended a practical management development programme. As the programme progressed the manager's skills increased and his sensitivity to the needs of others improved. Eighteen months after the end of the course his boss left. The manager applied for his boss's job, in competition with external applicants, and was offered the position.

## Case Study 5

The managing director thought long and hard about this problem. He recognized that he was messing other people around but also knew that he was not at his best first thing in the morning. His compromise was to make everyone aware he wasn't available first thing in the mornings, to schedule meetings for later in the day and to give his secretary advance warning of when he needed her to work overtime.

## Case Study 6

Consultants helped the team to work together, sharing each other's experiences. The consultants also enabled the team to take a step back and look at the whole organization and focus on profit rather than sales.

## Case Study 7

The physiotherapist's pilot scheme was so successful that she decided to incorporate therapeutic massage within the department's range of services. She found that patients tended to talk quite freely about their problems during their massages, so she decided to undertake a counselling course to enable her to respond appropriately.

Some common themes emerge from these solutions.

- Each involved a noticeable change of style which enhanced the 'emotional temperature' of their part of the organization.
- All the managers were aware of the need for ongoing feedback.
- Each recognized that managing people is a process of continuous learning.

# Assumptions

Charles Handy encourages us to look at the assumptions we use in our day-to-day work and to question whether they are helping us to achieve our goals or whether they are hindering our effectiveness.

Edgar Schein[1] helps us to understand these assumptions by calling them 'taken for granted' assumptions ('tfgs'). These are the attitudes and patterns of thinking that we have learned from our parents or guardians, our teachers, the culture we were brought up in, the culture we live in now and the organization we work in. Schein refers to them as 'taken for granted' because we rarely talk about them in our day-to-day communication yet they influence both our decision-making and the way we respond to other people.

These tfgs underpin our behaviour and can be illustrated as an iceberg, our behaviour being the part of the iceberg which

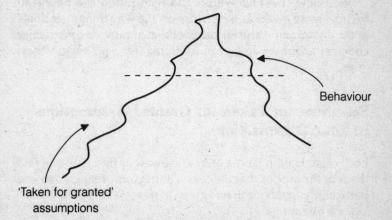

Behaviour

'Taken for granted'
  assumptions

is above the water, our 'taken for granted' assumptions being the part of the iceberg that no one sees.

This image is useful as it causes us to reflect on how much we know about our staff and our colleagues' tfgs and also how much they know about our tfgs. Continuing dialogue about individual and organizational tfgs within teams and between colleagues can help raise the iceberg further out of the water and can help clarity in communication and teamworking.

Often, because our assumptions are hidden, we don't pay attention to them or question them to see if they are still relevant and appropriate. Equally we tend not to be critical of our successful behaviours, unless we overuse a particular habit or strength.

Fritz Perls, founder of the Gestalt school of therapy, uses another powerful image in relation to our tfgs. He suggests that we look at all the assumptions we have ingested over the years and question whether they are still helpful to us now. If they are not, he suggests we metaphorically 'vomit them out' of our system and take in other, more appropriate assumptions.

This suggestion was made to help individuals but I think it is also equally important for organizations. Many organizations, particularly those that have been in existence for some time, have out-of-date or inappropriate assumptions which hinder their success.

Discussing this idea within an organization can help staff become more aware of the culture or 'the way things get done' in the organization and encourage them to provide constructive criticism about existing organizational tfgs and suggest new ones.

## Searching for Taken for Granted Assumptions in Your Organization

Each organization has its own unique set of tfgs. You can find them in the stories that are told within your organization and particularly in advice that is given to new staff. 'We don't . . . but we always . . .'

I have identified some of the tfgs I have come across in my work with a wide range of organizations:

We employ men as managers and women in support roles

Staff are dispensable; there are plenty of people who want to work here

Appraisals are carried out once a year and should take up as little time as possible

It's okay to lie to my support staff about deadlines, if it helps me get a sale

Our organization has a good reputation so we do not need to change the way we do things

We are helpless in the face of bureaucracy

No one ever gets sacked in this organization so you can do what you want here

All of these tfgs were hindering the effective management of people within those organizations. They need to be challenged. Now think about your own organization.

- Notice what people say.
- Look out for what they are also implying.
- Consider what advice you would give to a new recruit to help them understand those unwritten rules of behaviour within your organization.

Write down some tfgs which you have spotted underneath the surface of your organization.

1
2
3
4
5
6
7

Talk about these with your staff or colleagues and amend the list or add to it, as appropriate.

If you have a new member of staff in your part of the organization, suggest that he/she keeps a log of the different tfgs he/she hears, and then share the results with your team on a regular basis. Compare and contrast his/her results with the list you made. Some of the assumptions listed may be positive and some may be negative.

Over the years of consultancy with a wide variety of organizations, I have developed a list of seven Positive Assumptions which can help towards managing people more effectively. My Seven Keys to Success build on these assumptions (see chapter 5). Emphasizing these Positive Assumptions can help individuals and organizations to let go of existing negative assumptions.

## Seven Positive Assumptions

1. Managing people is about managing our relationships with other people.
2. Individuals can do anything they want to do – if it interests them. If they don't know how to do it they can learn.
3. Everyone has potential – in some people it is hidden and has to be identified by others.
4. Everyone is responsible for what he/she does and can be held accountable for it, provided he/she is given the appropriate authority.
5. We often have to let go of old habits before we can adopt new ways of doing things.
6. Everyone has his/her own view of the world and that can never be exactly the same as another person's, as he/she has not shared the same life experiences.
7. Everything and everyone is constantly changing.

I will introduce these seven assumptions individually, then talk about how to use them, and provide examples of people who have increased their effectiveness through adopting these new positive tfgs.

## 1. *Managing people is about managing our relationships with other people*

Helen Holmes, Chair of Bradford Women's Refuge commented:

*Managing people is actually about managing ourselves – Brilliant! This really helped me the moment I read it – not only professionally but personally too.*

Managers achieve results through other people. Managing the relationship between yourself, as manager, and your staff is crucial to your success. Managers have more power than they realize. Any result is a combination of an event and a response to that event.

Our behaviour is a tool which we can use to help or hinder our dealings with other people. Each of us has a lot of control in our relationships with others because we can control our own response to events.

Some people find it helpful to remember the following equation.

Event + Your Response leads to Outcome
$$(E + R = O)^2$$

This assumption confronts you with the fact that you are in charge of and responsible for your own behaviour. It also emphasizes that we do have power and that we can influence things.

Let's look at a common problem: participating in badly-run meetings.

*Badly-run meeting + No response leads to Waste of your time*

If you choose not to respond in the meeting you are colluding with others in wasting resources.

*Badly-run meeting + Your suggestions for change leads to Possible improvement*

Proposing ideas within a meeting challenges other people to help you solve this problem.

*Badly-run meeting + Negotiating your attendance for only that part of the meeting which is relevant to you leads to Saving your time*

This saves your own organization's resources and helps you to achieve the results you want.

We can modify other people's behaviour and attitudes through our own. As managers we often influence the motivation of our staff. We can choose whether we want to stimulate or temper their enthusiasm. For example:

*Being bullied + No response leads to More bullying*

*Being bullied + Talk to personnel leads to Potential change*

*Being bullied + Saying calmly but firmly 'your behaviour is inappropriate' leads to Change*

Using bullying as a method of providing a service of management to staff is a contradiction in terms.

In my final example the equation helps us to reflect on our attitude to mistakes.

*Mistake + No action leads to Bigger mistake*

*Mistake + Reprimand leads to Lowered motivation*

*Mistake + Positive response and rectification leads to Success*

How often do we respond to people who have made mistakes by saying: 'Just think about what you did', and have them focus on what they did wrong, increasing their guilt and possibly stimulating resentment? Wouldn't it be so much better to say: 'Think about the time last week when you did the same thing and got it right; what did you do differently then? How can we stop this mistake happening again?' These questions will help people to think about how to get things right the next time. The more specific we can be, the more it can help people to get it right.

# Welcome To a.c.t.

ANALYSIS CONSULTANCY TRAINING

We are glad to have you with our company.

Our number one goal is to:

> *Exceed* our customer's expectations

We have great confidence in you to:

■ Uphold our *Beliefs and Values*

## Belief and Values

■ Our personal integrity is precious
■ We treat others how we want them to treat us
■ We encourage the talents, individuality and beliefs of all people
■ We treasure our family life and leisure time
■ We have a positive attitude which helps ourselves and others to grow
■ We conserve the finite resources of the world
■ That for standing up for and behaving according to our beliefs we can influence other people
■ We constantly learn from experience

■ Set challenging goals that help us achieve our strategic goals
■ Help us fulfil *Our Aim*

## Our Aim

■ We work with our customers to improve people's performance in areas vital to the success of their business
■ By helping them to see more clearly what their people do now and how they can meet the demands of the future
■ We design and implement the best solutions
■ So that customers always want to work with us again, we earn a reputation for doing the best work in our field and so build a successful and profitable business
■ And all of us are proud of what we do for our customers, are well rewarded and develop personally through stimulating enjoyable and challenging work

■ Be scrupulously honest in everything you do
■ Challenge all assumptions
■ Focus on outputs not on inputs
■ Value all people equally, regardless of race, sex, religion or disability

ACT, a successful training consultancy, gives the leaflet on page 33 to all new staff and associates. They have created a statement of aims, beliefs and values which help new staff to get things right first time.

> *Give statement to new staff* + *Their response* leads to *Appropriate behaviour*

Does this actually happen in practice? Yes it does. I work with ACT and they are very stimulating to be with; they are expanding rapidly in a period of recession and are becoming very successful.

## 2. Individuals can do anything they want to do – if it interests them. If they don't know how to do it they can learn

This tfg was a revelation for me. A friend of mine had been brought up in a family that followed this assumption, whereas I had been brought up to be a 'nice girl', who doesn't climb trees, take risks, shout back, go to London etc . . . the list was endless.

These restrictions encouraged me to feel powerless and kept me constrained within an accepted pattern of behaviours. Inevitably I rebelled, but it has taken me many years to lose all my early conditioning and wholeheartedly adopt this assumption. I also know that my experience is not unusual and many other people feel similarly powerless and constrained by the 'messages' they received from their parents or guardians.

This assumption now helps me both personally, in setting my own goals, and also professionally, in working with others. It is useful when discussing self-development with an individual, as it widens the range of options available to them. Most people have limited aspirations for themselves, and in some cases for their families; this tfg challenges the limited nature of those aspirations. It also helps to guard against pre-judging people or colluding with other people's pre-judgements. Often people do not have to voice their prejudices for them to become apparent as you talk to them. A subtle one I encountered when talking about a particular manager went something like this:

> *He has tattoos on his arm and one earring; he can't possibly be a competent manager.*

Anyone can become a competent manager if they have the appropriate qualities and experience and if it is a job that interests them.

'*If it interests them*' is an important phrase in this assumption. What do you do if you want your staff to learn something new but they are not interested in doing so? As the old saying goes: 'You can take a horse to water but you can't make it drink.' Our job as managers is to gain the interest of the people we work with (the horse) and engage them in new ideas (make them thirsty), so that they will want to develop their skills (drink water).

It is often much easier to engage someone's interest if you talk to them rather than send a memo. The information that you pick up during a conversation can help you to identify what might stimulate this person's interest and help you work out how the project could be of benefit to them.

Staff are also more likely to be interested in doing things differently if the people around them are taking risks and trying new ways of working too, i.e., if there is a 'climate' which encourages learning and improvement.

## 3. *Everyone has potential – in some people it is hidden and has to be identified by others*

> *Performing below par and below potential may both stem from self-conditioning; the belief that failure and success are outside your own control can lead to failure for individuals and organizations; success can come from taking charge.*

Mark Brown in his article 'How to Create Success'[3] portrays these feelings of lack of control by talking about 'leafy managers', who feel as powerless as an autumn leaf falling from its tree, being buffeted hither and thither by the wind.

Very often the colleagues of 'leafy managers' are convinced that their managers will never change.

One of my management development programmes included several managers who worked for the same senior manager. The manager, who was nearing retirement, had many 'leafy' qualities, and this 'leafiness' was preventing the group developing, yet all his managers were convinced he couldn't change his behaviour and attitudes. We talked a lot about 'upward feedback', i.e., providing the manager with evidence that his actions were hindering improvements in service to customers.

The managers sought the help of their training manager, who facilitated team-building events, which enabled the managers, firstly, to present to their senior manager their evidence for his need to change, and, secondly, to plan improvements together in a constructive way. The senior manager enjoyed this process and is now an advocate for change: 'If I can do it, anyone can!'

We can change the way we view our abilities and improve our self-conditioning by using two simple phrases:

*I'm the kind of person who . . .*
I used to be the kind of person who was scared of computers. I told myself that other people had these special skills and I didn't. It was technical and I wasn't. Typing was not my skill; after all, hadn't I failed my Sight and Sound typing lessons, lulled to sleep by the metronome every time I took my eyes off the keys?

You can see how I talked myself into being the kind of person who was scared of computers.

Then I accepted a commission to write a book. Writing a book longhand is hard work – too much rewriting and cutting and pasting. So I decided to experiment and become the kind of person who found computers useful and interesting.

I am now giving positive messages to myself . . . I *am* the kind of person who finds computers useful and interesting . . . and it is becoming a self-fulfilling prophecy.

There are so many ways we can talk ourselves down into

a negative self-defeating spiral. 'I'll never . . .'; 'it's too hard . . .'; 'people like me don't . . .'

*Up Until Now*
If we change our self-talk to say I haven't done this, *up until now*, it allows us the possibility that we may do it in the future. The following children's poem describes how the phrase can help:

### Getting Up Courage

I haven't swung on rope swings
'til now
I haven't climbed up high trees
'til now
I haven't jumped into the pool
'til now
I haven't spoken French out loud
'til now
I haven't put my hand up first
'til now
. . . but I will . . . now!

We can encourage both ourselves and our staff to be more positive in the way we talk about ourselves and our abilities. We can also look out for that sixty per cent of potential, which John Harvey-Jones estimates people do not use.

## 4. Everyone is responsible for what he/she does and can be held accountable for it, provided he/she is given the appropriate authority

When I sent out these new tfgs to managers for their comments a number of them pointed out that many of the assumptions seemed too general and they wanted something more specific to relate to.

At the time, one of these managers was very frustrated with a colleague at work. There had been a recent reorganization and this colleague was not fulfilling his new responsibilities. The manager tried dropping hints, gentle persuasion and raising the matter in team meetings, yet nothing changed. The manager recognized that part of his frustration with his colleague was to do with the systems and practices within the organization. No one had clear and up-to-date job descriptions, so there was a lack of written clarity about who was responsible for specific tasks. There was also a culture of avoiding conflict so staff were often not confronted and held to account for what they hadn't done for fear of stimulating an unpleasant or angry response.

Clarity in responsibility and accountability are crucial elements of an effective organization. If responsibility is unclear, how can you give positive feedback on a job well done? Equally, if there is not an agreed system of delegation throughout an organization, how can you hold people accountable for what they are doing? (An effective method of delegation is described on page 80.)

You may not be able to reward your staff financially when they perform exceptionally well, but you can provide verbal or written thanks, access to training, responsibility for a special project, or perhaps some unexpected, additional time off. Frank Lord, managing director of Appleyard of Chesterfield, rewards his staff for solving problems, learning from mistakes, and achieving exceptional sales. On each occasion he formally presents the member of staff with a crystal goblet, in front of his/her colleagues.

## 5. *We often have to let go of old habits before we can adopt new ways of doing things*

Our typical learning process is described in the following diagram.

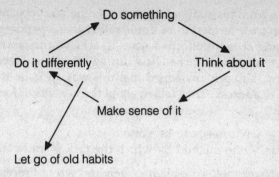

Many of us have to let go of old and comfortable ways of doing things before we can commit ourselves to trying new ways of doing things. Letting go of the old and familiar involves a feeling of loss. Learning to do new things often involves making mistakes, feeling uncomfortable and invariably takes a longer time.

The following simple model explains the process we go through when we learn something new.

*Unconscious Incompetence* → *Conscious Incompetence* → *Conscious Competence* → *Unconscious Competence*

We start off being unaware that we can't do something; then for some reason we recognize that we need to know how to do this but haven't got the skills; we acquire these skills but they initially feel new and awkward and demand more attention than our old, tried and tested skills; we become more comfortable with our new skills over time and come to feel relaxed about using them.

Identifying the potential benefits of change can help the process of letting go of old habits. For instance, in the long run, the change could save you time, give increased satisfaction, or perhaps transform your service or product and give you competitive advantage.

I mentioned earlier that it is possible to let go of a habit in thirty days, and I would like to illustrate how one person did this.

A manager working for a trans-national oil company received

feedback from his staff, which indicated he was focusing too much on *what* needed to be done, rather than spending time on looking at more effective ways to achieve the tasks. The manager talked with his adviser during his upward feedback interview, and acknowledged that this was an issue that he needed to address. They talked about the benefits of focusing on both

Task – what needs to be done
Process – the method by which the task is undertaken

The manager took a highlighter pen and wrote Process and Task in large letters in his diary for the next thirty days as a reminder to change his behaviour. He also included both Task and Process on the agenda of weekly meetings with his team.

Sometimes the fear of trying something new holds us back from changing our habits.

FEAR can stand for

Fantasized
Expectations
Appearing
Real[4]

Our vivid imaginations can dream up many reasons for not changing. If we let them. It is important to recognize that in many cases these reasons are not tangible or inevitable.

Another model which can help us to change is

## *I Have To Or Else . . . I Want To Because*

Think about some changes or tasks that are on your 'to do' list: particularly the ones that slip to the bottom and get transferred from one list to another. They probably fall into the *I Have To Or Else* category. List these in the first column. Then consider all the reasons you may want to do them: the results you will achieve, the satisfaction you will feel, the pressure that will be relieved; and rephrase your task in a second column, the *I Want To Because* category, incorporating those benefits.

I Have To, Or Else          I Want To, Because

Members of one organization I was working with were appalled when their chief executive said he would be visiting each section to look at the tidiness of the office, the filing systems and the use of space, prior to planning an office move. After much resistance to preparing for the visit, when staff eventually did the necessary tidying up it actually made their working day easier and they were able to locate things much more quickly. The above exercise might have helped them get started on the project more quickly.

## 6. Everyone has his/her own view of the world and that can never be exactly the same as another person's, as he/she has not shared the same life experiences

This is an assumption which celebrates the law of requisite variety and acknowledges the benefits accruing from diversity and difference. It can be helpful to us at a number of levels:

### Global

Many organizations are now planning and operating on a global rather than a national level. Such planning involves recognizing the diversity of a wide range of cultures and successfully integrating them within their operations.

### European

The cultural diversity of the people we live and work with is increasing. The mobility of individuals is increasing and regulations are changing, within the EU, to allow more people to work in countries other than their country of birth.

## *Organizational*

The people we work with and manage are, in most cases, of more diverse backgrounds than before. Many industries which traditionally did not employ women are beginning to do so. Women are increasingly achieving senior management positions or are setting up their own companies.

## *Personal*

Individuals are not as constrained by parental expectations or societal pressures as they used to be. Many people have a wider choice of job or career opportunities than previously and might change career as often as four times in their working lives.

Differences of any kind need not cause fear, but conversely, will more often enhance our work. If a team of problem-solvers have a rich variety of different backgrounds, they are more likely to create a *range* of possible solutions to any problem, however intractable that problem might be.

This assumption also helps me to recognize and listen to other people's points of view. It reminds me of Dina Glouberman's statement about a person's rights:[5]

I have a right to be who I am, feel what I feel, believe what I believe and want what I want.

I don't necessarily have the right to get what I want.

You have a right to be who you are, feel what you feel, believe what you believe and want what you want.

You don't necessarily have the right to get what you want.

You can value these differences by:

1. Sending 'I' messages and not 'you' messages; describe your own experience rather than labelling others.
2. Understanding the negatives and seeking out the positives in each situation you encounter rather than dwelling on either/or.

3 . Discovering the feelings behind the feelings. Ask yourself:
- What is behind this feeling?
- What did I feel just before I felt this?
- What is the original feeling?

4 . Accurate listening and assertive communicating.
- Accurate listening means you really listen and understand the other's point of view and acknowledge it as valid, whether you agree or disagree.
- Stating what you want assertively means that you really do feel that you have a right to your point of view and your needs as well.

5 . Separating me from you.

Be clear about 'what you want and feel, and what the other wants and feels'. Then be aware that there is no direct umbilical cord between you (even though it feels like there is), and that you can each learn to choose how to react to each other.

6 . Negotiating clearly.

It is important for each communicator to be specific about what they want from the other and to be specific about what they are willing to give the other.

7 . Locating what you have in common.

No matter how great your differences are with the person, it is usually possible to find out what you have in common and then to see the differences as variations in approach to the same goal.

Managers who are providing a service of management to staff and colleagues do not have an automatic right to get what they want simply because they are in a position of power. Their decisions must be based on need and circumstance and creating the best solution for their customers at that time.

## 7. *Everything and everyone is constantly changing*

In 500 BC the philosopher Heraclitus said, 'Everything flows and everything is constantly changing. You cannot step twice in the same river, for other waters are constantly flowing on.'

Yet we often try to design our organizations and make plans on the basis that things are static. Both individuals and the organizations which they create have two apparently contradictory goals: a longing for stability and a need for innovation and development.

Healthy cultures mix stability and innovation in the appropriate proportions. Regularity of structure, systems and task creates the familiar; yet these all need to keep in tune with the ever-changing environment in which we live and work. Acknowledging that everything is constantly changing means altering our planning, always allowing time and space for emergent strategy, and regularly reviewing plans in the light of changing circumstances.

Henry Mintzberg[6] illustrates such strategic planning in the following way:

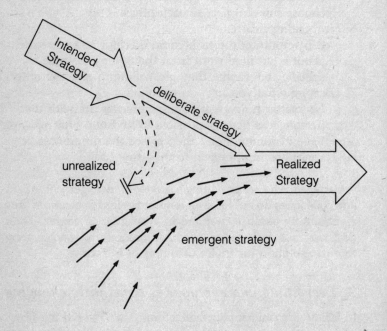

This assumption helps us, as individuals, to recognize that we are all constantly changing and growing. Our professional and personal life can be planned by giving ourselves achievable goals, within realistic deadlines. It can also be an adventure, responding to the unexpected or emergent opportunities which present themselves to us as we develop our careers and our lives.

## How to use these new positive tfgs

These new positive tfgs are written in universal terms as they reflect the way we tend to generalize our opinions when we talk about behaviours and assumptions.

Some managers respond to these new positive tfgs cautiously and say they cannot apply to everyone. They would have been more comfortable if, for example, the second new tfg had read: 'Individuals can do anything they want to do, *within their physical and mental limitations.*' I included this phrase within the tfg for a while and found that other people, particularly those with disabilities, thought that this was a 'cop-out' clause and it was not helpful. I know of someone, who was registered as a blind person, who chose to give up her disability allowance and went to train to be a teacher; I have worked with other people with multiple disabilities who are employed and do excellent work. I concluded that, within the context of people who were employed, the original wording was more appropriate.

My experience with all the new positive tfgs is that if you assume that people have these abilities and look for them, you begin to find them.

### *Applying them to yourself*

It is easy, in principle, to agree with these new positive tfgs. It is harder to apply them all in your work all the time.

Many people recognize that they use some of these new positive tfgs in their work already, so create plans to integrate the ones they do not currently use. My recommendation to managers is to adopt one new positive tfg at a time and make the learning a gradual process. If you adopt all these assumptions immediately, when you haven't encountered them before, they could move you beyond your 'comfort levels'. Some people enjoy the challenge of change and welcome that feeling of discomfort and disorientation; others prefer to avoid it.

## Applying them to others

When you feel accustomed to using the new positive tfgs within your own work, you can then encourage your staff and colleagues to adopt them also. Alternatively, you may decide to learn to adopt the new positive tfgs as a team, and use them as a definition of the way you want to work together in the future. Use of the new tfgs can be reviewed both in team meetings and supervision sessions and informal feedback can be gained from colleagues.

In summary, these new positive tfgs can help us, as managers providing a service of management, to broaden our outlook, develop empathy with our staff and colleagues, and release our own potential and the potential of others.

# Seven Keys to Success

This chapter describes a new approach to managing people. I use the metaphor of keys because it suggests several meanings: the *unlocking* of the skills and potential within you, and the opening of doors to new opportunities. This is one set of a manager's keys; other management competencies, for example financial management, create other sets of keys which join together to make one bulky keyring.

## Background to the Seven Keys Process

This approach starts from the assumption that there are three essential aspects that an organization needs to focus on:

   the needs of customers
   the needs of staff
   the needs of shareholders or members.

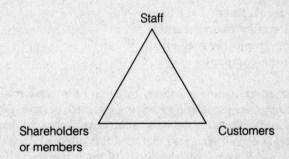

This model focuses on the needs of staff but does so in the context of the relationship to both customers and shareholders or members.

Recent research on managers and predicted future trends in management and organization development offer us new emphases and ideas about management. Peter Drucker[1] warned us in 1988 that the traditional role of the middle-manager was under threat, yet many managers continue in this role today. A new model for managers must be workable and durable and be able to be effective in fast-changing, turbulent times.

The Association for Management Education and Development and the Department of Employment undertook some research in 1991 entitled 'Developing the Developers'.[2] The purpose of this study was to identify the management issues that developers considered would be of high priority for managers in the future. The researchers asked developers what they thought would be the most appropriate methods and approaches for developing managers during the next five years. Their responses helped to identify the development needs of developers and also provided an insight into the future activities of managers. The top seven approaches were:

Team-building
Mentoring
Coaching
Self-development
Total quality management
Change/project management
Learning company.

In addition to looking at others' research I also undertook my own. Customer focus and providing a service of management to staff and colleagues were common approaches adopted by the good people-managers I met, and this fitted well with John Carlisle and Robert Parker's model[3] of the Integrated Effective Organization. This model is based on Total Quality Management principles and highlights an approach to management which incorporates the following features:

- Managed through a shared vision
- Systems designed to liberate
- Appropriate involvement and co-operation
- Customer-led
- Emphasis on quality
- Focus on long-term results

I was also attracted by another theory which focuses on empowerment. Maturana and Varela's theory of Autopoesis[4] argues that organizations do not operate in open systems where the external environment is acting down on the organization, as below,

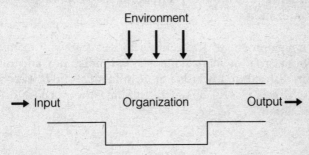

but in closed systems, with the environment being a part of a larger self-regulating system, as shown here.

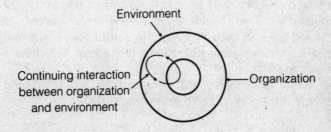

This distinction is important because it emphasizes that anyone within an organization can influence the way the environment – customers, suppliers, shareholders, the business community, the government, potential customers, etc. – react to that organization. And it will affect the way we manage people because it emphasizes that we can influence the environment we work in by our own actions, and that we all have more power than we realize. It highlights that:

*Managers have the opportunity to*

- Influence their staff and colleagues
- Influence their managers
- Influence their customers
- Influence their suppliers
- Influence the way the environment responds to their organization.

The development of these ideas moves us away from the traditional role of management as administrator and information-distributor, towards a more influential and far-reaching role which is closely linked to fulfilling the purpose of the organization.

# Developing the Seven Keys Process

The process of the Seven Positive Assumptions and the Seven Keys to Success was developed over a period of time and has been tested progressively by managers from a wide range of organizations. Two hundred managers were asked to implement them in their work and to send back results and suggestions for improving and refining the process, which have been incorporated.

The Keys to Success are designed to build on and complement the Seven Positive Assumptions.

## The Seven Keys to Success are:

> Clarity
> Customers
> Confidence
> Co-operation
> Creativity
> Commitment
> Choices

Each of the keys is equally important.

## *1. Clarity*

### *a) Provide clarity in all written and verbal communication*

Every manager I talked to recognized the importance of clarity and acknowledged that either they didn't communicate with other people enough or that other people didn't communicate with them effectively. When I heard this I was reminded of the research on communication which helped me to recognize why the issue of clarity in communication is often a problem within organizations.

When we communicate we use a combination of words, tone of voice and body language. Think about this when you communicate verbally with other people and assess what percentage of your communication is words, what percentage is tone of voice and what percentage is body language. Please write down the percentages below.

*Communication*

| | |
|---|---|
| Words | % |
| Tone of voice | % |
| Body language | % |
| *Total* | 100% |

Different research studies have come up with slightly different answers. The approximate percentages for verbal communication, taking these figures into account, are: words 7%; tone of voice 38%; and body language 55%.

Many people are very surprised by these results. However, it explains why telephone conversations can often lead to misinterpretation, as only forty-five per cent of our communication is being received by a caller. My own early scepticism about the figures disappeared after one particular incident, which highlighted the validity of these percentages.

I was on my way to a management development workshop when I was involved in a slight car crash. My car was still drivable so I was still able to run the workshop, but the group was getting off to a slower start than usual. It was only at our first break that I realized that while what I had been saying was fine, my body was still shaking like a leaf, and my tone of voice was decidedly wobbly. My communication was delivering very mixed messages to my participants. I should have had the wisdom to be honest about my feelings from the start, instead of 'putting on a brave face' and alienating the participants. Even if we often hide our bodies behind desks or computers they are still a part of our conversations and we can use them, and our tone of voice, to enhance rather than detract from what we are saying.

Research also shows that we tend to have preferred ways of taking in information. Each individual may have a different preference:

*Hearing* – people who like listening to information

*Seeing* – people who like to see things, or have facts written down

*Touching* – people who like to hold or handle things, or like to touch others as they talk

Identifying your own preference can help you to ensure clarity in the way you take in information; for example, if you like to hear things, meetings may be a better method of communication for you than memos. Recognizing your preference can also help you to prevent your communication being misinterpreted.

I shared this concept with a team which had a male manager and female staff. The manager recognized that he was a very tactile person when he was at home with his family and that although this was his preferred way of taking in information it was not appropriate in his workplace.

Looking out for other people's preferred ways of taking in information can assist in clarity of communication with others. People sometimes give clues about their preferred way in their conversation: 'I hear what you say'; 'You see what I mean'; 'I can't get a feel for that'. We need to be flexible in our styles of communication.

I was working with one organization where the chief executive was a 'feeling' person. Meetings with him were creative and relatively unstructured. However, when he moved to a similar role with a larger organization, his successor was a 'seeing' person. Successful meetings with this person were highly structured, with papers circulated in advance and little time for discussion within the meeting. Both meetings achieved the desired results. However if the same style of meeting had been used with both chief executives these results may not have been achieved.

The last important fact about communication is that we typically remember

$$\frac{1}{3}$$

of what is said to us.

In other words people forget two-thirds of what is said to them. Hence the presenter's phrase:

'Say what you are going to say; say it; then say what you have said.'

Skills of summarizing and clarifying are crucial within any kind of communication for they help to reinforce the central focus of the communication and give clarity about whether the information has been accurately received by all the parties involved.

## b) Show consistency regarding necessary confidentiality

Clarity about confidentiality is another very sensitive issue within organizations. Commitment to confidentiality may be linked to product, market, personnel issues, information about staff, customers, training or other matters.

Defining the limits of confidentiality can often be complicated – one person's commitment to confidentiality can be interpreted by another as secrecy or withholding information – so it is important to develop clear guidelines to prevent misinterpretation.

Clarity about confidentiality is also very important in supervisory, mentoring or counselling meetings with staff. In *Counselling for Managers* John Hughes[5] emphasizes that 'a ring of confidentiality' should surround any situation where a manager is counselling staff. He comments:

> *Only in the case of suspected criminal offence or intent, or if the lives of others are seriously endangered, should you consider breaking this rule; and only then to a responsible person (e.g. senior manager, doctor or police) after informing your colleague accordingly. It is probably wise to indicate at the outset that implied or intended threats to life, health or safety may constitute an exceptional clause to this general 'contract of confidentiality'.*

An old saying recalls that 'a confidence once betrayed is broken for ever'.

I vividly recall the occasion I was working in a personnel department and the chief executive congratulated a member of staff on getting a promotion, before he had been interviewed for the post. Not only was this bad personnel practice but it also caused all the staff who heard about the incident to revise their views about the competency of the chief executive.

In the absence of any formal guidelines any manager can adopt the 'do as you would be done by' principle. Employees have both a right to privacy and a right to know about how personal information kept on work files is handled. The interdisciplinary task force on privacy in Pfizer Inc., USA, created an eight-point policy statement for their organization:[6]

1. There should be no personnel information system whose existence is secret.
2. Information should not be collected unless the need for it has been clearly established in advance.
3. Information should be appropriate and relevant to the purpose for which it is collected.
4. Information should not be obtained by fraudulent or unfair means.
5. Information should not be used unless it is accurate and current, as well as relevant to the demonstrated need.
6. There should be a prescribed procedure to ensure that individuals are informed about the existence of information stored about them, of the purpose for which it has been recorded, and of procedures for its use and dissemination.
7. The employee should have the right to examine such information, and there should be a clearly prescribed procedure for an individual to correct, erase, amend or comment on information he or she considers inaccurate, obsolete, or irrelevant.
8. Any organization collecting, maintaining, using and/or disseminating personal information should ensure its reliability and take precautions to prevent its misuse.

Such a policy has many implications for personnel departments but can also be of relevance to managers. It poses a number of questions:

- Are your staff aware of where their personnel records are kept?
- Do they know if they have the right to look at them?
- When you are going to collect personal information from them, do you give them advance warning and explain clearly why you need the information?
- Do you allow your staff access to all the notes and information you keep about them?
- Do you record their comments on monthly review sheets or appraisal forms?

55

Some of these questions can be quite challenging to the 'traditional' manager who regards access to such information as solely a manager's prerogative.

## c) Maintain effective systems of information sharing

Some traditional managers tend to use knowledge of what is going on in their organization as power; they withhold this information from others. In contrast, other organizations may flood their managers with so much information that little of it is ever read. Creating a balanced method of information-sharing, which reflects the culture of the organization, is a complex task.

David Clutterbuck[7] describes one example of good practice: the Finnish building materials manufacturer Paraisten Kalkki. The organization believes that everyone in the company has a responsibility to the company and to their fellow workers to communicate as fully as possible.

> It issues every employee, from directors to the shopfloor, with a booklet outlining the duties to obtain and pass on information at each level of the organization. Informing the supervisor or employee representative on the works council about problems of work or about working conditions becomes part of the written job description. Communications can work properly, the booklet maintains, only if the employees take an active interest in the information and actively aim at informing not only others, but themselves.

For this to happen, the initiative and example needs to come from senior management.

Managers can also do a great deal, individually, to improve information-sharing in their part of their organization. This list was compiled from suggestions contributed by managers I have worked with. They found the following suggestions worked well in their organizations.

- Pass on all information as quickly as possible.
- Communicate face to face, where practical.

- Hold regular team meetings.
- Gain feedback and pass information up the organization.
- Manage by walking about and talk to staff informally.
- Ensure noticeboards are updated every two weeks.
- Keep memos brief and hand-written.
- Undertake quarterly quality reviews.
- Be approachable and have an open-door policy for a regular period each day.
- Maintain confidences and do not gossip, so staff will be willing to trust you with their problems.

## 2. Customers

*a) Recognize that you provide a service of management to internal and external customers*

Most staff in the majority of organizations know who their external customers are. However, many may not have thought about who their internal customers are. Charting your internal customer chains – the people between you and your external customer – can be an interesting process.

**Identifying internal customer chains within your organization**
I worked with one management team and several yards of different coloured tape and we physically 'modelled' their internal customer chains, using a different coloured tape for each major customer. We used the inverted triangle model (see page 16) and plotted the chains from the central focus of the external customer down through the chief executive to the shareholders.

Once we had established the chains, we focused on where there were blockages in the chains and whether decision-making was at the appropriate point along the chain, or whether it needed to be closer to the external customer. This was a complex exercise but it highlighted a major blockage, which people had previously thought of as a minor problem, and stimulated a significant discussion on the process of decision-making in the organization.

You can also undertake the same exercise on a large sheet of paper using different coloured pens.

### Identifying your own internal customer chains

Another useful exercise for individual managers is to focus on all the people within the organization with whom you have a significant relationship, i.e. your staff, your colleagues and your senior managers. By undertaking this exercise you might discover relationships with colleagues where there may not be a direct relationship within the hierarchy, but where you are dependent on their co-operation to get things done.

Take a piece of paper and put your own name in the centre; then write the names of your significant internal customers around the outer edges of the paper. These people include all the people you provide a service of management to. For example:

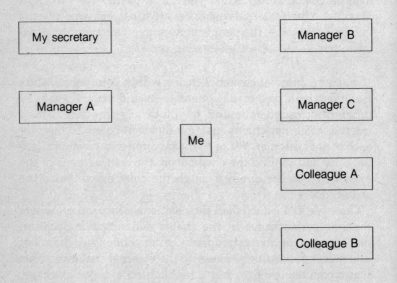

Then consider your professional relationship with each person that you have identified and decide whether this is:

Excellent
Satisfactory
Needs to be improved

If the relationship is

Excellent – join your name with a double line
Satisfactory – join your names with a single line
Needs to be improved – join your names with a broken line

The results may look like this:

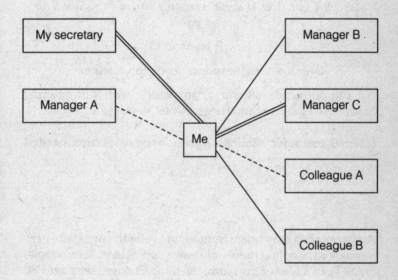

When you have recorded your perceptions of your working relationships, the next step is to check out those perceptions with your internal customers. If they do not accord with your view then you can discuss ways of improving the relationship between you.

Obviously, the chains that tend to be the most difficult to discuss are the 'Need to be improved' relationships. Using this model and talking in terms of improving your service of management to these people can help to keep the discussion focused on professional issues.

It is useful to fill in the following aide-mémoire.

List your significant internal customers in the first column. Then add your own rating (Excellent/Satisfactory/Needs to be improved) in the second column. Check out your rating with each internal customer, in turn, and note down whether they agree or disagree with your assessment in the third column. In the final column list all the ways you could improve each internal customer relationship. When filling in the final column it is helpful to remember:

*Managing ourselves is about managing our relationships with other people*

E + R leads to O

Event + Our Response leads to Outcome

We can influence all our relationships with our internal customers as we are in charge of our response to events.

**Internal customer   Rating   Agree/Disagree   Action needed**

Action needed may range from saying hello to your staff every morning to adopting more innovative approaches, for example, Frank Lord's idea of the Nominated Job Change (see page 99). You may gain other ideas for action from the examples of the seven managers in chapter 6.

### b) Design systems and structure to serve your customers/consumers/users

Your customers may have a variety of different titles. They may be referred to as consumers, users, patients, students, clients, providers or purchasers. For the purposes of this section we need to focus on the people who use or consume the service provided by your part of your organization.

Systems and structures are commonly designed to serve the needs of senior management, who were traditionally the decision-makers. If we reverse the 'triangle' (see page 16) we also need to look at our systems and structures to ensure that they are designed to help us to serve our customers, rather than hindering us in this task. As we do this we need to remember that these levers of change are interconnected.

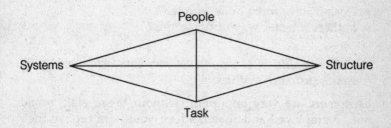

The Four Levers of Change

If there is change in one area it tends to influence one, or more, of the other areas. These changes may be positive or negative. It is important to recognize that there may be potential repercussions relating to any change that you consider, which act like ripples on a pond after a stone has been thrown into it. When planning it is important to be aware of this ripple effect so that you can create a system of feedback which accurately monitors what form the ripples take and where they are being experienced.

Philip Lewer provides us with a number of examples of how he redesigned his organization to meet the needs of the users (see page 106). Brewers Fare, part of the Whitbread group, responded to customer requests and improved their systems by providing braille menus in one of their pubs. Fortunately they constantly seek customer feedback and so were quickly able to recognize an oversight in transposing the menu. It said at the end of the menu 'Please see the noticeboard for daily specials'. The menu was revised and the braille menu is now available in all Brewers Fare pubs.

Many organizations are using 'Lean Production'[8] or 'Process Re-engineering'[9] concepts to reduce production time, error rate and cost, and so improve their service to customers. These initiatives need to be addressed on an organization-wide basis and are often beyond the scope of the individual manager. However the underpinning principles – to question and improve and integrate the processes we use – can be helpful to each of us. It challenges us to ask of everything we do:

- Is this process necessary?
- Does it have to be done as often?
- Is there a better way of doing this?

### c) Define quality in terms of customer satisfaction and gain constant customer feedback

Customers are very important; without them, staff would not be employed and shareholders would not receive their dividends. It is important to keep in regular contact with your customers as they are your 'quality controllers' and their comments will guide you and enable you to provide any service that meets their needs.

Managers are providing a service of management to their staff. They must, therefore, find appropriate ways of gaining regular constructive feedback from their staff. Many organizations have recognized the need to gain upward feedback from staff, in addition to the usual downward appraisal by line managers. Adrian Furnham, head of University College London's Business Psychology Unit, summarized the effectiveness of a number of schemes which focus on staff assessing their managers.[10]

> *In the UK, BP, British Airways and Central Television among others are changing their methods. Employees are not rated by their superiors but by their subordinates. Not top-down but*

*bottom-up. Simple and democratic though it is, the idea puts the fear of God into many managers . . . The bottom-up approach is the first step in the process of taking staff opinions seriously and allowing staff to influence the organization. The management toast for the successful go-ahead service-related business is a good one, not 'down the hatch' but 'bottoms up'.*

Cathay Pacific Airlines favoured this process of upward feedback for the following reasons:

- Subordinates tend to know their superiors better than superiors know their subordinates.
- As all subordinates rate their managers statistically, these ratings tend to be more reliable – the more subordinates the better.
- Subordinates' ratings have more impact because it is more unusual to receive ratings from subordinates. When communication flows up it is qualitatively and quantitatively different. It is this difference that makes it valuable.

I worked with Forum (Europe) when they introduced the Upward Feedback Process into BP Exploration in 1991. I was impressed by the way in which staff gave feedback to their managers and I was also delighted by the way some managers responded to their feedback and made significant changes in the way they did things as a result. The process was not a difficult one and it was often enhanced by gentle humour. Many managers felt much more valued as a result of the feedback they were given; they didn't realize that their staff appreciated some of the things they did.

## 3. Confidence

*a) Increase the self-confidence of your staff through delegation and providing continual constructive feedback*

If we are to release that sixty per cent of 'untapped potential' in our staff we need to encourage them to think, plan and act for themselves (whilst also providing them with appropriate monitoring and support). Managers can build self-confidence in their staff in a number of ways:

- by personalizing the way they communicate to staff
- by gaining information about self-confidence
- by using phrases which help to develop self-confidence

## Communicating to Staff

Jan Shutt of Sunday Best in Rossendale told me that she and her staff work together as equals and discuss everything together. 'I treat my staff in the way I would like to be treated. We spend a lot of our lives at work, so it's important we enjoy it. If we've enjoyed our work, we've enjoyed our lives.' Jan's fashion shops have developed an excellent reputation over the past twenty years and she has recently had her innovative ideas featured on TV.

But so often I hear of staff who are not treated like this. I was listening to someone talking about their chief executive. 'He gains external feedback on something I am involved in and doesn't bother to check whether the feedback is valid. He just metaphorically kicks me around the houses. My response is frustration, fear, freeze, and f\*\*\* off. I have stopped taking risks and just keep a low profile.'

Another similar reaction came from an employee who I heard saying, 'If she loses her temper I just turn off and stop listening to her.'

As managers providing a service of management, we can choose how we respond to events.

Event + Our Response leads to Outcome

A response of anger or aggression seldom creates the outcomes we want, in the long-term.

It is easy to de-motivate people; it is much more difficult to re-motivate them.

## What is Self-Confidence?

Defined simply, self-confidence is the sense of feeling and being *lovable* and *capable*.

Research indicates that one in three people suffer from lack of self-confidence; increasing the self-confidence of staff may therefore be a very important part of a manager's job. Our work environment can influence how confident we feel and how willing we are to take risks and improve our capabilities.

Think about yourself, at work, today. Estimate how high your self-confidence was this morning, on a scale of 1 to 10, as you travelled to work. Then assess how high your self-confidence was before you left work, at the end of the day.

If you find that your score dropped as you progressed through the day, or in response to one particular incident, you are gaining information about your own issues relating to self-confidence at work.

It may be appropriate to check with your colleagues or staff to see if they experience a similar drop in self-confidence. However, it may be difficult to find the appropriate opportunity to discuss the subject with others, in some organizations. Gloria Steinem[11] comments:

> *The idea of intrinsic worth is so dangerous to authoritarian systems (or to incompetent democracies in which some groups are more equal than others) that it is condemned as self-indulgent, selfish, egocentric, godless, counter-revolutionary and any other epithet that puts the individual in the wrong. If people feel they have a value that needn't be earned, the argument goes, how can they be made to work? Why should they continue to strive at all?*

Finding an opportunity to talk in such an environment may be difficult. Gloria responds to these sceptics:

> *To answer this question, we need only remember that it is in infancy and early childhood, the period where we are most likely to feel unconditionally loved, that we learn and stretch our abilities more than at any other time in our lives. No one had to reward us for learning to roll over and crawl, or penalize us for not standing up or walking. We didn't need orders to explore the world around us, or a competition to say our first words. These things were learned from the sheer joy of accomplishment,*

> *stretching our own abilities, choosing what we wanted to do*
> *and then doing it, the surest path to good work at any age.*

She concludes:

> *People who are worried about laziness and the work ethic need*
> *only look at examples of chosen work versus compelled work,*
> *or work for which we feel personal responsibility and pride versus*
> *that done in an anonymous group. The truth is that, like every*
> *other part of nature, human beings have an internal imperative*
> *to grow.*

Managers who are providing a service of management are, therefore, like gardeners. It is their job to develop an environment in their part of their organization where staff have the right conditions to grow and develop.

We can influence our environment by the phrases we choose to use and the attitudes we take. If we strive towards having an open and positive approach to our work and enhance this with constructive phrases we create good conditions for growth.

Everyone is doing the best they can, *at the time*

I often adopt this phrase as a ground rule in problem-solving and team development workshops. It recognizes that people generally want to do their best; however, there are times when due to reasons such as lack of time, resources, health etc., they do not do as well as *they* want to, or as well as *you* want them to.

Using this phrase is not a way of avoiding doing something, or a method of condoning poor performance. It is a way of highlighting that there is an issue which needs looking at, without getting into blaming. It recognizes that things need to be done differently next time and that this planning can be done with an objective emphasis, rather than a subjective one. It offers the manager the opportunity to say 'What can I do to help you to get it right next time?', and helps to create high-level compromises and solutions, rather than settling for either/or superficial low-level compromises.

Remember also when you judge yourself harshly that you are also *doing the best you can, at the time*.

Another phrase that can be helpful when you or your staff have received negative or aggressive criticism is:

*No matter what you say or do to me I'm still a worthwhile person.*

I knew someone who worked in an environment where they were regularly and repeatedly criticized, for no real cause. They chose to say this phrase over and over as they drove to work each morning to help them to retain their self-confidence.

**Feedback**
We can also influence our environment by the way we give feedback to others. Negative feedback is the most commonly used form of feedback and yet it is the most demotivating for the recipient. Making a habit of giving positive feedback, when a job is well done, can be a great motivator for staff. Alternatively, if you find that things are not as you wish them to be, provide feedback which is constructive. Constructive feedback means saying what you don't like and saying what you would prefer. Check out the way you give feedback against the following points:

*Feedback needs to be* informative *rather than* evaluative.
By informing the other person about the effects of his or her behaviour on you, the recipient remains free to use the information or not; it provides an option. By avoiding the use of evaluative language, you reduce the other's tendency to respond defensively. You might say, for example: 'I haven't finished speaking yet', rather than, 'You're ignorant to interrupt me like that!'

*Feedback needs to be* specific *rather than* general.
Describe the particular behaviour you are observing rather than talking in vague, broad or inconclusive terms about to the behaviour. For example, to tell someone that they are 'dominating' will not usually be as useful as providing them with a description of their behaviour. You might say for instance: 'Just now, when we were discussing this issue, you

67

did not seem to be listening to what others said, and I felt forced to accept your statements or face an attack from you.'

*Feedback needs to be* tentative *rather than* absolute.
A person who appears to be taking a provisional position tends to communicate to others that they, too, may have some 'say so' in what happens. The individual who, in giving feedback, responds with absolute statements seems to be saying: 'I have all the answers and I know they are correct.' It may be more appropriate to say: 'You seem unconcerned about what happens' rather than 'You are rude and enjoy putting people down'.

*Feedback needs to be* checked out *against the perceptions of the recipient.*
Always summarize what you have said, to check that the recipient has interpreted the feedback correctly.

*Feedback needs to be* shared *at the* earliest possible *moment.*
The earlier the feedback is given, the more helpful it is likely to be. The opportune moment will, of course, depend on a number of factors: the willingness and readiness of the individual to listen and hear the feedback; the degree to which the atmosphere feels supportive; and the degree of trust that each person has for the other.

*Feedback needs to be* constructive.
Tell the other person how you want things to be different.

*Feedback needs to be both* positive *and* negative.
We often tell each other about what we don't like; it is helpful to provide a balance of both positive and negative constructive feedback.

## b) Have the self-confidence to recognize, acknowledge and sort out difficult situations

Many factors can make dealing with difficult situations daunting, for instance: having staff who are older or more experienced than you; being under time pressure or working to unrealistic deadlines; being inexperienced in dealing with situations of conflict. In addition, some organizations have a culture of avoiding conflict.

Conflicts take time and sensitivity to resolve and so are sometimes left unresolved, pushed 'under the carpet'. Frequently the conflict does not go away and the lump under the carpet simply gets bigger and intrudes in a more significant way, which damages good working relations.

Conflicts, like mistakes, are always easier to resolve when they are small. Here are a few principles which can help us to deal with difficult situations or conflicts:

- Conflict isn't bad.
- Conflict will stir our emotions and that's okay.
- Not all conflicts can be resolved . . . or at least not by me, at this instant, with my resources.
- We are all different; we respond differently to conflict, with different 'trigger points' and different ways of expressing our distress.
- It helps to deal with conflict when it first occurs. If you 'brush it under the carpet', it tends to grow in size and complexity.
- There is no magic formula for handling conflict. Developing an awareness of what's right for you and what's right for the other people involved in the conflict is helpful.

Try practising these skills when you find yourself in a difficult situation:

### Naming
Be clear and honest about the problem as you see it, stating what you see and how you feel about it. Use 'I' statements: 'I see . . .', 'I feel . . .' This ability to name what seems to be going on is crucial to getting the conflict out into the open, where we can begin to understand and try to deal with it.

Seek the best time to do this. Do not avoid it, for it needs to be done.

69

## Listening

Listen not just to the words, but to the feelings and needs behind the words; listen without judging, without the quick automatic response, 'I know how you feel.'

It takes a great deal of time and energy to listen well: reflecting back, asking for clarification, asking for time to be listened to, being truly open to what you are hearing (even if it hurts), being open to the possibility that we might ourselves be changed by what we hear.

## Opening up

Open up to the possibility that there may be other solutions to this conflict in addition to those you have thought of so far. Open up to your imagination, creatively exploring the range of possible solutions available.

Set aside time and attention to brainstorm ideas/solutions with all the people involved in the conflict. Involve them in agreeing the most appropriate solution.

Use the 'head, heart and guts' test to get in touch with your intuitive feelings. Relax yourself and close your eyes. Think about the proposed solution. Centre your thoughts around your head and note the response. Then centre your thoughts around your heart and note the response. Lastly centre your thoughts around your guts/stomach area and note the response. If all three areas agree you have intuitive approval for your plan. If there is disagreement, this will give you further information about your proposal.

Any agreed solution will need monitoring to see if it is appropriate in practice, needs minor changes, or is influenced by new unforeseen events.[12]

### c) Seek new ways of doing things, take risks and do things differently

Continual learning involves being constantly aware of the possibility of there being different or better ways of doing things. It is sometimes hard to focus on doing things differently when we are very busy. Many managers find that it helps to set aside ten minutes each day to look back at what they have done during the day and consciously plan for the next day.

Planning to do things differently can be influenced by our attitude to change; if we see change as an adventure, which is exciting, we are far more likely to want to change than someone who sees change as a threat.

If you are convinced about the need to do things differently but are hesitant about changing, the following phrase[13] can be helpful:

'Oh What The Heck, Go For It Anyway'

Sometimes when we take a risk and try new things it can have amazing results. I thought about this phrase when I first contacted John Perkins about seeking permission to use his quote from the *Financial Times*. The worst he could say was no. He responded by saying that he was happy for me to use it, *and* also invited me down to Heathrow *and* asked what he could do to help with the book. If I hadn't taken the risk of contacting John I would have missed some excellent material.

When you have done things differently and they have worked, then celebrate your success. Keep a success file and/or share your success with others. I took John and the other six 'Day in the life of' examples (see chapter 6) out for dinner when we had completed our task. We had a memorable evening where each of us sparked ideas to and fro.

## 4. Co-operation

### a) Work to agreed ways of operating with your staff

There is a myth that the 'killer instinct' is necessary to survive in the business world. Many organizations are moving away from this traditional viewpoint and find that co-operation enhances learning potential, whereas competition tends to discourage making time to learn.

Alfie Kohn shows us in his book *No Contest: The Case Against Competition*[14] that in all his extensive research he could not find evidence supporting the view that competition was helpful. In fact he discovered that competition

- Is inefficient
- Kills curiosity
- Undermines genuine love of learning by focusing on external gain
- Creates anxiety and need for approval
- Makes us suspicious, hostile, envious and contemptuous of losers
- Destroys self-esteem
- Poisons relationships

Many companies in the field of information technology are developing strategic alliances with competitors. The health service is recognizing that the purchaser/provider relationship can only work well if it is approached in a co-operative way. The oil industry survives because of its 'symbiotic relationship' with specialist contractors.

The benefits of co-operating can be highlighted by these simple equations:[15]

$$\text{Little} \quad + \quad \text{Little} \quad = \quad \text{Bigger}$$

$$\text{My vision} + \text{Your vision} = \text{Our vision}$$

Co-operation is important for managers who are providing a service of management because they are trying to work *with* their staff, rather than *against* them, and are wanting to develop the right climate for their staff to grow. One way of creating a 'climate for growth' is to spend some time discussing and agreeing the way you want to work together.

The arrival of a new chief constable allowed South Yorkshire Police the opportunity to clarify their shared understanding of working together and working with the community. The following statement was created after widespread consultation inside the organization and with the public. It was then sent to each member of the South Yorkshire Police with a personal letter from the chief constable, backed by action plans from line command. This statement was tied into disciplinary procedures and career development assessments to ensure greater effectiveness. The document was also distributed widely to the public.

---

### South Yorkshire Police
### Statement of Purpose and Values
(Extract)

**Our Way of Working**
In upholding these fundamental values, it will help us to be more effective in working together and with our communities if we:

- Maintain the dignity of our office yet display humanity and compassion.
- Constantly practise high standards of personal and professional conduct.
- Remember that, although the office of constable carries power and authority, respect must be earned.
- Listen and try to understand the other person's point of view.
- Confront those who bully or exploit on behalf of those less able to protect themselves.
- Act with a willingness to try new ways of working.
- Speak moderately, yet firmly and proudly, of what we do well.
- Admit our failings promptly and apologize for our mistakes.
- Show determination and resourcefulness in helping others.

---

Such statements are not public relations exercises. They provide the opportunity for staff to use the statement as a 'benchmark' against which to measure their performance. They are also helpful as a 'benchmark' if a colleague or their boss is not working to this standard, as the statement provides a non-confrontational way of discussing their lack of performance.

73

## b) Ensure men and women work effectively together

I have co-facilitated many workshops on men and women working together effectively. At the most recent workshop we ran, our participants were volunteers from a cross-section of one organization; there occurred a very interesting dynamic. Split into single-gender groups, participants had been exploring 'messages' that they had received from their parents or guardians when growing up. There were more women than men in the workshop, which gave an opportunity for comparison and discussion within the gender groupings. One group of women considered that these 'messages' had been let go of and were not evident in the workplace today. The other group reported back that few of the 'messages' had been let go of and they created problems in their workplace, at present. Both groups worked in the same organization.

I use this example to illustrate that ensuring that men and women work together effectively is a complex issue. It goes beyond equal opportunities policies and equal rights in promotion and being regarded, by yourself and others, as someone of equal value. It does not mean that men and women are the same; this approach recognizes that they are equal and different. They have been 'programmed' differently as they were growing up. Many women and men have chosen to reject their early messages and adopt different attitudes; others still retain traditional beliefs.

We all possess so-called 'male' and 'female' characteristics within us (although some would prefer to deny it). So it is important for each of us to recognize and value those 'characteristics' and to use a balance of them in our day-to-day work.

As a manager providing a service of management you may find it helpful to discuss these issues with your staff and your team to ensure that your work is not being hindered by any unnecessary misunderstanding between the sexes.

## c) Developing long-term customer–supplier relationships

Many large organizations, for example Marks & Spencer, develop 'preferred supplier relationships' as a way of ensuring consistency in the quality of their products. Other organizations, for example Levi Strauss,[16] issue global sourcing guidelines to set out new terms of engagement with suppliers and retailers and exclude those operating in countries with 'oppressive' regimes.

Nicky Keogh, of Keyo Agricultural Services (see chapter 1), decided to put these principles into practice and set about 'growing' his own supplier. He approached one of the company's ex-employees and offered him, free of charge, any support necessary to establish himself. He is so successful now that Nicky wants him to agree to train others.

If we can let go of the myth about competition and recognize that there is much to be gained by co-operating, we may spot similar opportunities for growth. Involving suppliers, whether they be providers in the health service or specialist contractors in the oil industry, can help you to improve your service of management to customers.

## 5. Creativity

Lots of people talk about being creative; few people are actually creative, in practice. Gareth Morgan explains why, in this humorous listing of ways to kill creativity.[17]

### How to kill creativity

- Always pretend to know more than anybody around you.
- Police your employees by every procedural means that you can devise.
- Run daily checks on the progress of everyone's work.
- Be sure that your professionally-trained staff members do technician's work for long periods of time.
- Erect the highest possible barrier between commercial decision-makers and your technical staff.
- Be certain not to speak to employees on a personal level, except when announcing rises.
- Try to be the exclusive spokesman for everything for which you are responsible.

- Say yes to new ideas, but do nothing about them.
- Call many meetings.
- Put every new idea through channels.
- Stick to protocol.
- Worry about the budget.
- Cultivate the not-invented-here syndrome.

He concludes: 'Note the relationship between these managerial attitudes and practices, and the everyday functioning of many bureaucratic organizations.'

Managers who provide a service of management to their staff need to examine their part of their organization and see if any of the elements described above are in existence. Any procedure which is hindering creativity needs to be re-examined, amended or, if necessary, abandoned.

*a) Use mistakes as learning experiences to improve service*

What is your reaction to the word 'mistake'?

'Oh, I'm terribly sorry I made a mistake'

'We don't pay people to make mistakes'

'If you don't make a mistake you don't make anything'

These are all common responses; the first two discourage creativity; the third encourages it. Many organizations do not actively encourage creativity. 3M, however, has developed an 'eleventh commandment' which says:

'Thou shalt not kill a new product idea'

Post-its are one example of a 'mistake' which has become a very successful range of products.

The learning and development process requires people temporarily to be at a loss (see Incompetence to Competence model, page 39), and making and eliminating mistakes is part of the process of creating the appropriate product or service for customers. So, we need to gain constant feedback from both our internal and external customers and the environment in order to identify and rectify mistakes as quickly as possible. Small mistakes are always easier and less expensive to resolve than big ones. Don't allow mistakes time to grow.

## b) Encourage and reward initiative and innovation by your staff

This idea was described in some detail in chapter 4. If we, as managers providing a service of management, give positive feedback on successful initiatives taken by our staff, we increase the likelihood of their wanting to take risks again.

## c) Develop your team and gain ideas through shared problem-solving

Several heads are better than one: managers can improve the quality of their decision-making by using their team to brainstorm solutions to complex problems.

I have found that the following method is particularly successful for drawing out and prioritizing a range of solutions to a complex problem.

### A creative way of brainstorming using Post-its

1. Everyone writes down their ideas about the problem on Post-its (one idea per Post-it) without discussion.
2. Each person puts their Post-its on the flipchart in turn. No one comments until the last Post-it is in place.
3. Remove Post-its where duplication occurs.
4. Discuss and develop ideas.
5. Group Post-its into themes or possible solutions. Check everyone agrees with these groupings.
6. Create headings for the themes or possible solutions using different coloured Post-its.
7. Arrange themes in order of priority.

This method

- Is democratic – everyone contributes
- Is participatory – everyone puts Post-its on the chart and moves them around

- Is quicker than other approaches
- Is more flexible than 'traditional' brainstorming
- Creates high quality decisions
- Can be used by the team whenever there is a problem; doesn't need a facilitator
- Is also fun to do.

## 6. Commitment

### a) Value your staff and recognize their different talents

Providing a service of management means working with your staff in an 'I'm okay; you're okay' relationship, where each values the other. Some traditional managers used to work in an 'I'm okay; you're not okay' relationship, where they assumed that they knew best and would 'tell and sell' their answers to their subordinates. Such a style of management would often produce reactions of submission or aggression from employees.

When we are providing a service of management we are encouraging our staff to be assertive and state their views and share their ideas for change. In order to do this we need both clarity and equality within our relationship with them.

Some staff like to keep their work lives and their home lives separate and choose not to talk about their hobbies or their families; others enjoy talking about their other interests. I find it interesting to hear about managers' activities outside work as they often have talents developed in leisure time which can be very useful at work, yet have not been explored in the workplace. One manager I was working with did a lot of work with youth groups focusing on positive-thinking and self-confidence. When we talked about these ideas he suddenly became aware of how he could use his skills with his own staff at work.

Valuing staff also means going beyond stereotypes and relating to each staff member as a unique individual, with a unique and special range of skills and experience. Positive assumptions six and seven are particularly relevant to this point (see pages 41–5).

*b) Ensure that you and your staff are committed to acting responsibly. Hold people accountable for what they do*

Acting responsibly means ensuring you are carrying out your responsibilities in the following general areas:

- Towards your customers
- Towards your staff
- Towards your suppliers
- Towards shareholders/council
- Towards the broader community
- Towards the environment.

In this sense you are providing a service of management to a very wide range of people.

Consumers are becoming increasingly interested not just in the products or services they buy, but also in the behaviour of the company or brand and the way the product or service was developed.[18]

Premier Beverages, a division of Premier Brands, launched its fair trade initiative in February 1993. It selected plantations on social and environmental criteria and placed the 'Caring for tea and our tea pickers' logo on all Typhoo tea packaging. In December 1992 Timberland, the shoe manufacturer, ran an advertising campaign against racism (Give Racism the Boot) in the US and Germany in partnership with charitable bodies to emphasize their stance on racism.

In a narrower way you are also ensuring that your staff act responsibly if you hold them accountable for what they do. The Delegator's Dozen[19] describes a comprehensive framework for successful delegation. I have used this system of delegation with several organizations. It works best when:

- Everyone in the organization uses the same system
- All the steps are followed, all the time
- It is used consistently over a period of time.

## Delegator's Dozen[19]

1. Set a clear objective.

2. Select the delegatee:
   a) ask for volunteer
   b) match task with type of person.

3. If necessary, train the delegatee.

4. Get input from the delegatee. Gain their ideas.

5. Assign task/project *and* deadline.

6. Provide necessary guidance on
   a) any critical information or data that delegatee must know
   b) suggest different approaches
   c) describe results required or set standards.

7. Make a delegation contract and identify levels of authority appropriate (may be multiple levels in a task or project)
   Level 1: take action
   Level 2: take action but stay in touch
   Level 3: get approval before moving on
   Level 4: do only what I tell you to do.
   (Aim to get all employees to Level 1.)
   Identify controls: budget limits and recruiting limits.

8. Establish system of monitoring (but do not meddle).

9. Review regularly; reinforce accountability; praise the behaviour you want repeated; don't take the responsibility back. If there are problems, ask for:
   a) a clear statement of the problem
   b) an evaluation of the alternatives
   c) recommendations.

10. Provide feedback.

11. Identify lessons learned.

12. Evaluate performance and give recognition for a job well done.

This looks, at first glance, to be a complex, time-consuming process. It doesn't have to be. Once you have memorized the twelve steps and used them every time you delegate for a period of one month, they become a new habit and will then take seconds rather than minutes.

Photocopy this chart and stick it on your office wall in a place where you will look at it frequently. When you reach point 8, check you have delegated a) responsibility, b) authority at the appropriate levels, and c) accountability.

The distinction between responsibility, authority and accountability is important. Give clear responsibility to a named individual for completing the task within a realistic deadline. Make sure you have also delegated appropriate authority, i.e., to spend money and involve others. Be aware that you can never delegate total accountability – that remains with you and means that you have to answer to others when things go wrong; so it is in your interest to monitor progress regularly. If things do go wrong then 'the buck' stops with you; if the project is successful you may want to give public praise to the delegatee.

Experiment each week and delegate to someone you have never delegated to before. Stimulate your staff to move beyond their 'comfort levels' and take responsibility for new tasks, on a regular basis.

## c) Show commitment to the goals of your team and the purpose of your organization

Developing goals for the way you work as a team can help in building your team and in clarifying what you have in common. One of the MENCAP teams in Yorkshire has recently created a statement of team/home goals.

---

**We work**

to give our residents the best possible standards of care
and a better standard of living

**We aim to do this by**

being honest, assertive and accountable and working to
Quality Assurance standards

working as an effective team and understanding
each other's roles

reviewing our practice through regular supervision and
undertaking appropriate training

continually improving information flow and giving
communication a high priority

**We value**

time together as a team which helps us to understand each
other's needs and be more tolerant of each other's opinions

positive thinking and giving credit to each other's
achievements.

---

When the team originally formulated this statement they recognized that it was a statement of how they wanted to work; it was not how things were working, at the time. The statement was posted on the wall so everyone saw it all the time and staff made a commitment to try and work to that standard. Three months later they reviewed the statement in a team development workshop and unanimously agreed that their goal had become a reality.

## 7. *Choices*

*a) Recognize that you can influence outcomes as you are in control of your response to events*

Every experience is a chance to learn, yet we don't always learn from every experience. We can influence outcomes as we are in charge of our own responses (see page 31).

Event + Our Response lead to Outcome

However, there are times when we don't feel able to implement or communicate our response. In such situations we tend to feel powerless and need support, but often we are met with an opposite reaction.

Gaining some understanding of how people react when they are feeling under pressure can help us to guide them back to a situation where they feel able to respond and make choices. One model that can help us to do this is the concept of

W Activity
and
S Activity

W Activity – 'work' or 'whole' activity.

S Activity – 'survival' or 'splitting' activity.

W Activity is mental activity characterized by attention to task, role and achieving objectives in realistic time spans.

S Activity occurs when external circumstances stimulate an unconscious internal mental threat which arouses anxieties about the individual's ability to respond adequately to the external demand, e.g., making a difficult decision or learning a new role. The resulting anxiety causes the individual to re-direct his/her energy from the longer-term W task to the task of defending the self. Defence mechanisms, for example projection, rationalization and splitting (dividing the world into heroes and villains), are commonly a feature of S activity.

If an individual is involved in S activity and is preoccupied with defending his/herself, it can be difficult to communicate with them about a task linked to W activity. It may be necessary to resolve the 'real' underlying problem relating to S activity before communicating about the 'presenting' problem or issue relating to W activity. When the situation regarding 'S' activity is resolved the person may then feel able to re-engage with W activity and recommence communicating his/her choices and influencing their world.

## b) Regard issues not as puzzles which have one right answer but as problems which have a range of solutions

Puzzles are like sums or a jigsaw: there is one right answer or one correct place for each piece. Some of the issues we deal with as managers are puzzles, but generally those which are associated with managing people are not puzzles but problems.

Problems are complex issues which involve the need for knowledge, questioning and making judgements. Problems always have a number of possible solutions and the range of options needs to be identified, explored and evaluated to identify the most appropriate solution for that problem at that time.

Making this distinction when managing people is very important.

The implications of this for managers are:

- Problems need reflection time to draw out the range of options available, prior to decision-making
- Additional knowledge may be needed to explore the issue
- Consultation or discussion with interested parties may be necessary
- Problems are specific to time, place and person/s; you cannot automatically apply a solution that worked in one situation to another similar situation
- Check personnel procedures and legal implications of all your possible solutions

- Look for creative options which may not have been considered before
- Examine the problem from different angles until you see it as an opportunity.

Many people draw back from spending time creating solutions, for they feel overwhelmed with the problem. They may feel uncertain about whether they are able to deal with the emotions that are linked to 'people problems', and find it hard to gauge the appropriate emotional temperature. But, as Nicky Keogh (see pages 5–7) found, staff are often more resilient at times of crisis than we expect. After talking about the company's crisis with his management team Nicky was able to agree redundancy without rancour and provide those staff with appropriate support.

An important question to ask is:

> *Do I allocate sufficient 'quality time' to undertake this brainstorming and problem-solving approach in my day-to-day work?*

Time management experts tell us that things take fifty per cent longer than we expect them to. Do we sometimes get sucked into treating problems as puzzles due to a shortage of time?

## c) Transform problems into opportunities

Every problem can be transformed into an opportunity if you 'walk round it' and view it from different angles. Recognizing that any current issue can be 'labelled' as either an opportunity or a problem can help us to change the way we view the issue and respond to it.

One manager brought what she felt was an enormous problem to an Action Learning Set I was working with: she hated the assistant director of her company and felt completely paralysed when they sat in management team meetings together. Her guilt about this was increased as this person was credited with bringing the company back into profitability and she felt that she ought to feel grateful to him.

85

The other set members helped the manager to put her situation into perspective. Initially she had regarded the assistant director as being 'as big as the room': a problem so big she felt she could never resolve it. She eventually recognized that the assistant director was metaphorically 'as big as the sugar basin' and that although he had excellent strategic skills he was very lacking in his ability to relate to others. The manager recognized that she had gained new insights and saw the problem as an opportunity to share skills with the assistant director; for she was skilled at the things he was not, and vice versa.

# 'A Day in the Life of'
# Seven Effective Managers

With any approach it is easy to say that it 'looks great in theory'; what is more important is how it works in practice. These 'Day in the life of' profiles illustrate the way the Seven Keys to Success work in practice. They are intended to:

- Stimulate you to identify what you can do to change your working day
- Provide practical examples
- Create a similar experience to that of 'shadowing' the manager
- Represent a wide spectrum of different organizations
- Describe managers in a range of different work environments
- Illustrate innovative ideas
- Use the managers' own words.

It was a delight to work with these managers in creating a 'typical' day. These 'typical days' describe real events and are set within the time span of each manager's average working day. Some of them are fictitious in as much as the events mentioned didn't occur together within the same day. They are condensed so the reader can gain a wider appreciation of each manager's innovative ideas and approaches.

# A Day in the Life of John Perkins, Chief Engineer, British Airways

## *Personal Profile*

After undergoing engineering training in the Royal Air Force and rising to the dizzy heights of junior technician, my military career was cut short by a road accident which left me minus a right leg. I joined BOAC as a tradesman in the electrical workshops in 1956 and, having obtained my first aircraft licences, left there in 1958 to join British European Airways as an electrical inspector. After nearly ten years of this interesting and varied life, I was asked to take over the engineering aspects of our operational control and ran the maintenance control operation for BEA for some six or seven years. During this period, the final mergers of BOAC and BEA were taking place and I played a key role in merging the two control operations into one. We went through the very painful process of reducing the engineering workforce from 14,500 to 8,000 while the company as a whole struggled with a twenty-five per cent cut in its workforce. It was a time to stand up and be counted or get out.

In 1982 Alistair Cumming came on the scene from Rolls-Royce, as the new director of engineering. I consider myself to have been extremely fortunate in being picked out by Alistair, who moved me rapidly up the management ladder, culminating with my appointment in 1986 as chief engineer of aircraft maintenance. This is where all the real work finally got done in bringing the company into the 1990s. I worked very hard with a group of consultants and some of my colleagues in restructuring the organizational shape of engineering so as to remove a layer of senior management (mine) and a supervisory level.

## *Organizational Profile*

The engineering division of British Airways is recognized worldwide for the quality of its product and the technical innovation which the company has always subscribed to.

Increasingly, it is becoming known now for its sound business base and the way in which it can deliver value for money to its customers both inside and outside the airline. It is frequently held up as a model inside British Airways of the way in which change can be achieved without war, and as an example of management style which has been able to change from an autocratic one to one in which people genuinely do work together. The Total Quality Management ethic has been embraced within British Airways' engineering management in a very successful way and one which will undoubtedly prove, in the long-run, to have been its salvation.

## A Typical Day (circa 1992)

07.30-09.00. *Co-operation*. Meeting with major national consultancy group to discuss restructuring the engineering organization. I want to be sure that we can work together to produce a plan for restructuring the organization, which the people involved in will support. It is essential that my people have confidence in our achieving the end result.

09.00-12.00. *Creativity*. Chair a SMART Steering Group (see page 13). Members of the group are keen to find new and creative ways of problem-solving and create the necessary savings on money and recruitment. I am impressed by the way members of the group have developed into a team and work effectively together. The SMART idea arose out of the Margin Improvement Steering Group and I shall enjoy giving positive reports on our progress to this next meeting.

12.00-13.45. *Choices*. Act as engineering representative on the Margin Improvement Steering Group. This is one of a series of meetings of representatives from the key divisions of British Airways. The problem we face is to find savings of £200 million across the company and there are no predefined solutions. The engineering contribution to this is some £47 million and a great deal of creativity is required to obtain the necessary savings. We are provided with sandwiches to encourage our creativity.

**13.45-14.15.** *Commitment*. Took dessert and coffee with the Inspections Standards Course. This course is designed to improve technical performance and record problems. I helped attendees to understand what the external view of the regulatory authorities is, and gave them the facts about how we compare in terms of quality. I also updated staff on a number of issues. This was an opportunity for me to highlight my commitment to the course and to support the people who were running it.

**14.30-16.00.** *Customers*. Quarterly meeting with our flight operations colleagues to review how we were doing in terms of supplying them with the services they wanted. The improved technical performance of the aircraft was very much what they had been seeking over a period of some years, but they were disappointed with some of the trade-offs we had done in terms of not carrying out work which they considered essential. It was an opportunity to look through not only how we were getting on, but how the interfaces worked between the two groups.

**16.30-18.30.** Drive to Warwick.

**19.30-22.30.** *Clarity*. Evening meeting over dinner, a one-to-one, very confidential discussion with a full-time national official of one of our engineering trade unions. The purpose was to discuss very far-reaching plans to restructure most of the group. The plans would involve the total dismantling of the structure which he represented at national level, and in fact would result in him having no significant presence inside British Airways engineering, following these restructuring plans. While absolute clarity was necessary in order that there could be no misunderstandings about what was wanted, the meeting had to be held in a climate of absolute confidentiality. Not only was he never to indicate in subsequent negotiations that he had prior knowledge of what was going to happen, but no one else in British Airways knew of the action I was taking either. This was a high-risk position to say the least.

---

**John**

- Asks staff where savings can be made

- Seeks creative solutions through teamworking

- Monitors customer satisfaction through quarterly meetings

- Supports training by his commitment to contribute to key courses

- Uses 'benchmarking' to improve performance and compare quality

- Involves the union in early discussions about changes

- Highlights the importance of shared values when working with outside agencies

---

## A Day in the Life of Maggie Stubbs, Primary Care Manager, Sheffield Community and Priority Care Services

### Personal Profile

I enjoy nursing and have been involved with this profession since leaving school. I have practised in hospitals and within community units in different parts of the UK as a district nurse, midwife and health visitor.

My B.A. Hons degree course in 1987 motivated me towards striving for a managerial post within nursing, and in 1989 I became clinical nurse manager with Sheffield Community Unit. Continuing my professional development was important to me and I chose to complete a Masters degree in business administration. This helped me in my management role by giving me a good platform on which to build my management/business skills and expertise.

91

Recently I have been promoted to the post of primary care manager, a move away from an operational level to a more strategic focus. My work involves managing resources and human resource accounts for more than half of the total budget. I gain particular satisfaction from working in this post because it has taken me a lot of time and money to get there; I had to fund myself on the first two years of my degree course; gaining a scholarship from a baby food company paid for my third year. As a single parent, I didn't have much money to fund myself through my MBA. I chose to remortgage my house to enable me to complete the final year of the course.

I like to think that I act as a role model for other black employees within the health service. It is important for them to see that black people can study and take risks and be ambitious within the health service and achieve success.

## Organizational Profile

The core business of my organization is patient care. Its principal objective is health promotion, disease prevention, cure and caring for health. Our aim is to provide integrated, speedy and efficient treatment and care for everybody, but with a particular emphasis on the most vulnerable and needy in our society.

The Sheffield Community Nursing Services Unit serves a population of 528,300 within an area of 143 square miles. The unit is organized into several directorates, one of which is the Nursing and Patient Care Services Directorate and all the nurses and health visitors are managed within this. This unit is facing a period of major reform in an environment of significant change brought about by the National Health Service (NHS) reforms, political uncertainty and demographic factors.

Our unit is beginning to operate within a business-type arena as a provider to the District Health Authority (DHA), the Family Health Services Authority (FHSA), general practitioners, fundholders and the purchasers. The unit has recently registered its intention to move towards trust status. I am enthusiastic about moving to NHS trust status as we should enjoy more freedom in determining our strategies and plans.

## A Typical Day

**08.00-08.45.** *Clarity*. Check my diary to remind me of the day's plan. Check post of previous day, this includes NHS circulars, minutes, training schedules, and sort into order of priority. Action urgent mail and place remainder in the reading file. Check signing file and action these. I then prepare for the fortnightly management meeting by rereading the previous minutes, looking at the action column and identifying the actions to be taken and by whom. I then finalize the agenda and prepare items to be discussed.

**08.45-09.00.** Check my diary with my secretary to note any appointment changes. Ensure all appointments are made that need to be made and try to prioritize these according to diary space.

**09.00-12.00.** Management meeting with my clinical nurse managers, sector administrative officer, senior nurse and personnel officer. This meeting takes place fortnightly and is the formal arena for two-way information sharing. It is often difficult to stay within the time limit because this is our opportunity for clarification. There are written minutes which are used as an aide-mémoire. The information from this meeting is then taken by managers and delivered to the relevant staff.

**12.00-13.00.** *Customers*. Meeting with the co-ordinator of Acute Intervention Initiative (Hospital at Home). This is a pilot project being developed to prevent certain older patients from actually being admitted to hospital. They are nursed at home with extra nursing input. Check the budget allocated against the equipment ordered for emergency use. Discuss marketing exercise undertaken with GPs, selling the idea to them. Arrange awareness sessions with members of the Primary Health Care team to try and gain their support. Plan to attend an information gathering day in Peterborough about Hospital at Home. Set date for next meeting.

13.00-13.30. Lunch at my desk, returning urgent phone calls and sharing a joke with my secretary.

13.30-14.30. *Confidence and Choices*. Individual fortnightly meeting with one of my clinical nurse managers. This is an opportunity for each manager to discuss issues affecting their locality, i.e. staff shortages and staff training. It is also a chance for me to provide feedback and for us to discuss individual performance and personal development. Each meeting has a positive focus with an agenda compiled by both the clinical nurse manager and myself. I take notes as an aide-mémoire for us both.

14.30-15.30. *Co-operation*. Visit to GP practice that has applied for GP fundholding status. The main focus of the meeting was on collaboration and creating a new way of working in conjunction with GPs and practice staff. Discussion with the Practice Clinical Nurse manager regarding the contract with the Community and Priority Care Services Unit for purchasing of Nursing and Health Visiting Services. In-depth discussion on historical activity levels and the perceived activity levels for the future with the new system of contracting in place. Clarification was sought on cover for sickness and annual leave for the attached staff. The question of practice staff involvement in future recruitment and selection of new community unit staff was on the agenda but this needed a protocol. A good understanding and a shared agreement was reached, and a date was set to discuss these issues with the staff concerned.

15.45-17.00. *Creativity and Commitment*. Meeting with two health visitors running a Sleep Clinic. This was a new initiative they had developed and piloted. It involved providing advice and support to parents with toddlers who were having sleeping problems. Referrals were made by health visiting colleagues and there were eight sessions lasting over two months for each group of clients.

The first two sessions involved exchanging information and

the others were more on the lines of self-help. All participants kept a diary mapping their child's sleeping patterns and noting improvements. The pilot period was evaluated and proved successful. It showed improvement, mainly in the parents' coping skills. This present meeting was mainly to have an update on these sessions. We also needed to find a more suitable venue that was permanent and more accessible by public transport. Discussion also took place about ways to fund a day's seminar on sleeping difficulties in children.

17.30. Look at diary to remind myself of the following day's work. Look at message pad and pick up reading file to read at home in preparation for meetings or actioning the next day. At the end of the day I allow myself time to reflect on the day's activities, evaluating the objectives achieved, reshaping and rescheduling those that were not achieved and questioning the way issues were handled, what was learned and planning improvements for the next time. Following the Demming Quality Model: I plan, I do, I check and I act.

---

**Maggie**

- Spends time preparing for meetings

- Uses meetings for two-way information flow

- Works collaboratively to establish a successful purchaser-provider relationship

- Encourages staff to develop new initiatives in response to the needs of customers

- Monitors performance through fortnightly positively-focused meetings with each of her managers

- Uses pilot projects to create new services for customers

- Reflects on her activities at the end of each day

---

## A Day in the Life of Frank Lord, Managing Director, Appleyard of Chesterfield

### Personal Profile

Initially when I was asked to give an objective profile of myself, I was reminded of what James Russell Lowell (1819–1891) was once quoted as saying:

Whatever you may be sure of,
Be sure of this,
That you are dreadfully like other people.

My background is from a large family of four sisters and a mother and father who worked all hours possible to give us a good education. In my case they failed. They did, however, lead by example and gave me a set of balanced values that have been central throughout my life.

At the age of twenty-seven, I decided that I wanted a general management position. Up until then I had worked as a district manager for a motor manufacturer and as a line manager in the retail motor trade. At night school, I studied for my diploma in management studies, and then a Masters degree in management studies, and more recently the MIPM qualification.

My leadership is strong, enthusiastic and demanding and my management style is open, accessible and flexible. I encourage initiative, respect human nature and, like all managers, I do not communicate effectively enough.

### Organizational Profile

Appleyard of Chesterfield started trading as a Peugeot franchise in February 1989. We began with no customers, a handful of staff, and an investment in land and buildings of £1.3 million. At the time our parent company, The Appleyard Group PLC, considered this their most important project. We soon developed a clear vision: 'to be the best Peugeot dealership in the country'. Our mission statement, known as the 'Appleyard Promise', breathed life into the organization and has shaped the values and determined our culture ever since. This culture, which puts customers and the staff who serve them first, has been crucial for our drive towards 'Total Quality'. In the last four years we have achieved BS5750 accreditation, and the Investors in People standard. Appleyard of Chesterfield has quickly developed all areas of its business to become the leading Peugeot dealer in the UK, winning the coveted Gold Lion Award three times in succession. As a result of a recent employee development initiative, the organization has declared itself a 'learning company'. A learning resource centre, known as ALEC, the Appleyard Learning and Education Centre, has been set up and is uniquely staffed by a team of non-managers.

Having a clear vision, not compromising our values, and investing in our people has provided the following concrete results for the business:

1. Low staff turnover.
2. Low absenteeism.
3. Clear and shared vision.
4. Customer satisfaction index well above industry average.
5. High morale.
6. High customer retention.
7. High customer referral rate.
8. High profile with local community.
9. Mutual respect of staff and management.
10. Right First Time – continually improving.

## A Typical Day

08.10. *Choices.* To succeed, every business has to have action; action is based on decision-making, and decision-making based on choices. Today, before making a decision on a staff disciplinary matter concerning a line manager, I asked myself, 'What choices do I have with this person?'

Previous disciplinary procedures concerning this individual have been necessary, and everything looked as though it was set to follow the same pattern. However, this time I decided to turn this situation on its head. I asked myself two simple questions: 'Taking into consideration the "total" contribution of this person over a continuous period of time, is their performance reasonable, consistent and predictable? Will the organization continue to prosper and develop with them as a central part?' My answer to both questions is a definite YES! The meeting that followed was unusual; the meeting was turned upside down!

The disciplinary warning that was expected didn't happen. Managerial rights were not exercised; rather, they were replaced with duties, which said:

1. Your contribution to the long-term success of our business is critical.
2. Your overall performance and quality of work and relationship with others is high.
3. How can we learn from a recent bad experience and is there anything I can do to help?

We both left the office from our 'upside-down' meeting with our feet firmly on the ground. The experience had strengthened rather than weakened our relationship.

09.30. *Creativity*. The manufacturer whose cars we sell undertakes customer research from time to time in the form of using actors to call us up, pretending to be actual customers. Each conversation is scored out of a range of pre-set questions and compared to the national average. The sales team do not like to be measured in this way because they see it as a threat. I am in receipt of the latest report showing that we are falling behind in certain areas and that although we are not below average there is room for improvement. Usually I send some of my staff on a training course. Normally the improvements come, for a period, and then tail off until I get a report from the manufacturer and then start the whole process off again.

This time, though, I search for a creative alternative and remember that one of the sales team is on a management development programme and is in need of a project. Calling the team member into my office we explore a creative new approach which results in the following course of action:

1. He will act as team leader for the sales team in reviewing their level of customer service on all incoming sales enquiries.
2. The sales team, under his direction, will review the entire procedure. Their proposals will include the whole process, including response times from the main switchboard.
3. The method of measurement will be by using an outside company to telephone in eight times a week over a period of three months.
4. The sales team will present their findings and future proposed action after the three-month period.
5. I will not be involved in listening to any of the recordings or reviewing any of the data.

When he left my office I felt more comfortable with this new creative approach, and more excited about its potential outcome.

10.25. *Co-operation*. An unscheduled meeting with our administration and accounts supervisor highlights a particular problem; he requests a 'Nominated Job Change'. Nominated Job Changes are requested by staff when the output from someone else is causing them difficulty in completing their job. They request that the particular person works with them for a day to see the problems they are causing. I talk with the sales person who has been 'nominated' to work in sales administration for a day and arrange a date for the Nominated Job Change. This approach helps to improve relationships and develop staff awareness of how their job affects others in our internal customer chains.

11.00. *Clarity*. A new technician has started today and his line manager has been busy with his induction. As they enter my office I am acutely aware that the few minutes I spend with this new member of our team will be critical. It is a wonderful opportunity to show consistency from our earlier meeting at the recruitment stage. I remind him about what the company stands for and how central the 'Appleyard Promise' is in terms of the business being totally customer driven. I am passionate in the way I express my views and I provide the utmost clarity in emphasizing the values of our business and stress that they are non-negotiable. I explain to Peter that his job is vital to the success of the business and that I will be taking active interest in his achievements.

11.20. *Commitment.* I attend a short meeting with the ALEC team (Appleyard Learning and Education Centre).

One of our six business objectives is to develop all our employees. ALEC was born from the result of an attitude survey which highlighted that at least half of the company's employees did not know how to find out about the training or development opportunities open to them. Six non-managers took on the responsibility of developing the centre and funding was obtained from N.E. Derbyshire TEC. ALEC is proving to be a very successful employee development initiative as every person in the company has taken up some form of vocational or non-vocational learning. ALEC has just become operational as a centre and needs some repairs to the building, which also needs decorating.

I am called to this meeting to be asked if the repairs and redecorating can be paid for by the company or if it will have to come out of the ALEC budget. To endorse my commitment to the initiative, I agree that the company will support the repair expenses to allow ALEC to invest in people.

11.45. *Confidence.* Seeking new ways of doing things and taking risks in doing things differently is firmly built into the culture of our business.

I meet with Devon, a painter, to review his training and development plans. Devon wants to develop into sales so he works during the week in our accident repair centre and at the weekends as a sales person in our car showrooms. I took the risk of developing his ambitions. As a business, it gives us valuable help at our busy times (weekends) and it also gives a clear signal to everyone in the company that we have confidence in our people and are willing to try out new ways of doing things.

Our meeting is to discuss Devon's training and development plan for the next six months and to give constructive feedback on how he has done in his part-time sales job for the past three months.

12.25. *Customers*. Lunch with ten internal customers in the Learning Resource Centre.

13.00. Team meeting focusing on feedback from our external customers. These team meetings happen three times a year for every employee. Constant customer feedback data (internal and external) is presented to the team from the following sources.

1. Attitude surveys.
2. On site customer surveys.
3. Customer questionnaires.
4. Customer panels.
5. Mystery shopping surveys.
6. Job change.
7. Manufacturer surveys.

The company is split into mixed groups of eight to ten and the feedback is discussed in detail. Success is evaluated and ideas for improvement are generated. These meetings typically generate forty ideas for improvement and today is no different. Our mission is to continually delight our customers. All the ideas are included in an action plan and reports on progress occur regularly between meetings.

17.00. I draw the team meeting to a close by saying, 'It's nice to end the day focusing on customers, as it reminds us all that without customers we have no future.'

---

**Frank**

- Motivates staff through a clear, shared vision

- Chooses an alternative solution to disciplining staff

- Delegates creative problem-solving to a team member

- Resolves problems using the 'Nominated Job Change'

- Inducts a new member of staff stressing that the values of this business are non-negotiable

- Develops a learning organization through ALEC

- Evaluates success and generates ideas for improvement during quarterly team meetings

---

## A Day in the Life of Kath Attenborough, Business Strategy Unit, Employment Service

### Personal Profile

Before joining the business strategy unit, I worked in a wide variety of fields within the Employment Service: marketing, training, corporate planning and budgeting. In recent years, I have studied for an MBA; other relevant knowledge includes fluent French and passable Italian. The linking factors throughout my eighteen years of employment are a focus on the labour market, and caring for the people I work with. I now run a small team in the business strategy unit, working on a wide range of short-term projects. These include designing and delivering an international conference, European briefings, reviewing IT strategy for local offices and value for money issues.

### Organizational Profile

The Employment Service was created in 1987; its central aim, taken from the mission statement, is to 'provide an effective and high quality public employment service'. Now a Next Steps Agency within the Department of Employment, it has undergone — and is still undergoing — a considerable cultural change. 'We will become a business-like agency, respected for the quality of our customer service and people.' Ways in which it is trying to live out its message that 'The ES serves people through people' include working towards the Chartermark and Investors in People standards.

The business strategy unit was created in 1991 as part of the re-organization of head office into directorates. The aims of the unit are supporting and improving the co-ordination of initiatives, developing marketing and external relationships, and considering European issues.

## A Typical Day

At a working seminar for senior government officials from European countries.

08.00-09.00. *Co-operation and Customers*. Discuss with project leader today's administrative arrangements; ensure a vegetarian option is available at meal times; see if enough money remains in the budget to pay for a guided bus tour of Edinburgh this evening; check the implications of last night's decisions about today's programme for coffee, meal times and location of meetings. Then ask reception to accommodate the necessary changes (they are wonderfully accommodating!). Glenys, one of our facilitators, offers to book the bus tour.

09.00. *Clarity*. At the French translator's request, I sit next to her just in case there are any technical terms in English of which she is unsure.

10.30-11.15. *Confidence*. Whilst acting as facilitator during the first of the small-group discussion sessions, I recognize that there is a need to control some of the contributors in order to stay within time constraints and to give everyone an opportunity to speak. Managing translated contributions is never easy.

*Creativity*. One of the delegates produces diagrams explaining how advisory and counselling services operate in his country. These are quickly put to use as the focal point for the rest of the discussion.

*Commitment*. We could keep introducing new issues for another hour. However, the task is to bring the group to agreement on the three most important issues to emerge. We do so (the only group to finish on time) with the offer that, if we wish, we can continue this discussion over lunch or later in the bar.

13.00. *Co-operation*. Am approached by the link facilitator to discuss the running order for the afternoon's presentations. We reach a jointly-agreed order in thirty seconds flat.

15.30-16.30. *Choices*. It is clear that having spent much of the day listening to presentations in a second language, a number of the delegates are beginning to flag, despite their obvious interest. I drop a hint to the organizer, adding that the interpreters are also getting tired.

16.30. *Confidence*. Someone requests a five-minute break. When the link facilitator hesitates, acutely aware that we are running behind schedule, I comment that the break will help us all to concentrate and listen better to the remaining presentations. We take a break.

18.00. *Co-operation*. Am asked by Glenys if I am prepared to provide whispered translation into French during the guided bus tour this evening, so that we can give our hard-working and exhausted interpreters the evening off. The interpreters and I check with the delegates concerned that they are happy with this. (Someone comments that I am a workaholic.) The other facilitators offer to help out over dinner and later in the evening.

18.30-19.00. *Choices, Creativity*. Meet other seminar organizers in the bar to discuss how to run the final morning. The link facilitator outlines the structure: sessions to be replaced by working groups, because the second opportunity for discussion yesterday disappeared in a long working day with people's exhaustion. I offer to take the group on the strategic design of a counselling and guidance service since I have a methodology for tackling that. Also suggest a topic where a natural group seems to have emerged during the seminar, and suggest how Glenys can still use her prepared notes with the third working group despite all the changes to the programme. We go into dinner content, I think, with the way things will run.

*Commitment*. After the heady re-organization of the final day, we pause to check that the changed programme will still contribute to achieving the objectives set for the seminar.

19.00-20.00. *Customers*. Sit between the French and Italian delegates at dinner to ensure they can join in conversations in the absence of our interpreters. A facilitator colleague does a wonderful job in fluent Italian.

20.00. *Clarity and Co-operation*. During a guided bus tour of Edinburgh I provide whispered translation from English into French. Even translate the sexist remarks, although I add my own comments, making it clear where I am doing so.

21.00. *Confidence*. Talk with other organizers in the pub about various consultancy techniques: the use of complexity and chaos theory in economics and management, and the power and range of systems theory as a tool in facilitating both small groups and whole organizations. These discussions are interspersed with others on the state of labour markets elsewhere in Europe, the economic benefits of counselling services and the situation with regard to equal opportunities in the UK and abroad.

22.00. *Customers*. Ask several of the delegates what they thought of their bus tour. They very much welcomed the break and wanted to see more of Edinburgh on the final day if possible.

---

**Kath**

- Seeks regular feedback from delegates
- Ensures that the specialist needs of delegates are met
- Incorporates new ideas into discussions
- Focuses her group on the key issues
- Responds flexibly to delegates' requests
- Initiates changes in the programme, after consultation
- Creatively amends the programme, ensuring it is still meeting the original objectives

---

# A Day in the Life of Philip Lewer, principal officer, Community Mental Health Services, Bradford

## Personal Profile

My management style dates back to my time as a market stall holder when I was fifteen in 1967/68. I tend to be open, straightforward and honest; my aim is to delight my customers.

I started my professional working career as a trainee social worker in 1970, moving to this 'proper job' from that of a weaver in the cotton trade and a petrol pump attendant. Six years after qualifying I became an area officer, my first management job. If I was a good manager as an area officer, it was by chance rather than by design.

When my job developed and I was responsible for a budget of £2 million and some 200 staff, I really felt I needed some more training. The part-time MSc in management was a wonderful opportunity for me, and Lancaster University was like a breath of fresh air, bringing together all my thoughts and allowing me to redirect my energy. I felt refreshed and renewed and able to take on the bureaucracy that was around within local government. I shared ideas with the managers who were responsible to me, so that they were creative and responsive in providing a service that met identified service users' needs.

## Organizational Profile

I joined the Department of Social Services in Bradford in 1977, and have stayed because I have enjoyed the place and the people. Enthusiasm and commitment are encouraged at all levels, and progressively managers' time has been freed to encourage creativity. The department has approximately 4,500 staff and a budget of approximately £57 million. In September 1992 I was appointed assistant director, and I now have approximately 3,000 staff (mostly women) and a budget of £19 million.

Massive changes are being instituted by central government as Care in Community, driven by the NHS and Community Care Act 1990, became operational. I believe that this is a wonderful opportunity to demonstrate the strength, commitment and enthusiasm of the workforce in providing the high quality of community care services in fierce competition from the independent sector.

## A Typical Day (early in 1992)

07.00. Record my overnight thoughts on my dictaphone as I make a cup of tea for my family. I have three dictaphones, one for the office, one for the car and one that I carry with me. As I drive to work I replay my dictaphone thoughts from the previous evening so that by the time I reach the office I have clarified my key issues for today.

07.45. Arrive at work, check files for day ahead, prepare for meetings and time-manage my day so I have both thinking time and recuperation time.

08.30. *Commitment*. Meet with the staff at one of our hostels to discuss their recommendations for improving the conditions of service for staff. (We felt we could improve staff conditions.) I cannot increase pay but many staff, particularly those returning to work after a career break, would like to work more flexible hours and their current contracts do not allow this. Their recommendations include part-time staff working on a rota for ten hours per week but arranging their remaining five hours each week at a time which suits both them and the hostel. They also suggest that generic job descriptions would also provide greater flexibility. I thank them for these excellent suggestions and agree to share them with other staff. (Both of these recommendations were subsequently implemented and were very successful. Our staff turnover and absentee rates have also greatly reduced.)

09.00. *Clarity*. Lengthy phone conversation with users of our service who want us to establish a one-stop telephone number for all our services. This could operate from 10 a.m.-10 p.m. every day and would need to be provided in more than one language. I agree to research the cost of such a service. These service users also identified that they had a number of training needs. They recognized that they needed training in assertiveness, managing meetings, public speaking and a session on how our department works. So they would feel able to participate effectively in defining appropriate services for the future. We agreed that Saturday would be a good day for the training as it didn't conflict with other commitments.

09.45. Time to exchange information and events with my secretary over coffee.

10.00. *Co-operation*. Meeting to discuss the accommodation needs of people with mental ill health. Representatives from users, NHS Hospital Trust, Health Authority, voluntary organizations and advocacy projects are present. We agree to set up a project group to research needs and make recommendations. Members of the project group include a representative from each tier of the department. We discuss the complexity of the group's task and allocate the group twenty hours' time and a deadline of two months. The group members can decide how they want to use this time: whether in day or half-day meetings or shorter, more frequent meetings.

11.00. Time to record thoughts on dictaphone and prepare for next meeting.

11.15. *Choices*. Meeting with manager from NHS Hospital Trust to finalize the arrangements for a joint database, ensuring that we are targeting our resources at those most in need. This is the final step to improving our allocation system and having systems in place to measure the service. Previously, this process could take up to six weeks and involve up to twenty people. When the joint database is functional, we will be able to make a decision in ten minutes.

12.15. Sandwich at desk. Record thoughts on dictaphone. Return urgent call.

12.30. *Creativity*. Drive to see our new Renault Espace. The final deal was negotiated by a unit manager with the help of users. They managed to reduce the purchase price by £3,000 by encouraging the garage to advertise their name, in red letters, on the back of the vehicle.

13.00. Drive the Espace to three of our establishments to collect users who wish to attend the Mental Health Forum.

**14.00.** *Customers*. Facilitate Mental Health Forum. This is the power-house which drives our service. Its purpose is to ensure that our service is accountable to the people who use it. This group set the performance indicators for our service. Once a month an informal meeting is held for users, voluntary agencies and invited staff, from the Local Authority and the NHS Trust at an independent location.

I start this meeting by reporting back on action in response to user requests to keep our day centres open at weekends. I then ask for requests for the agenda. We start by hearing about the progress a voluntary agency is making towards registration as a charity. If they can become a charity they can apply for increased funding and offer more services to our users. I offer help in working through this process and we set a date to discuss it. I encourage user queries and I am asked, 'Can you catch mental illness from toilet seats?' No. 'Then why are there separate toilets for staff and users?' This turns out to be a question addressed to the NHS Trust but I make a mental note to double-check our services to ensure we don't still have the remnants of such policies in existence. A representative from the NHS Trust responds to the question. We work through our agenda, stopping for a break for tea.

**17.00.** *Confidence*. Drive users home and stop and have a chat with a unit manager. He talks enthusiastically about the changes he has made since he has been delegated the authority to manage the budget for his establishment. Each unit manager can now move money between different budget heads if this helps to provide a more customer-responsive service. This unit manager has bought a personal computer for the establishment. He has put all his budget on the computer in such a way that his users can call up the budgets on the screen and obtain information about budget-spend to date.

Record my thoughts and ideas on the dictaphone I keep in my car as I am waiting at traffic lights on the drive home.

**Philip**

- Reassesses and simplifies existing systems
- Changes conditions of service to meet the needs of his staff
- Delegates authority for managing budgets to his unit managers
- Involves service users in decision-making
- Uses short-term project groups to research needs and make recommendations
- Establishes joint databases to improve resource allocation and communication
- Records his ideas, and reflects on them, using dictaphones

## A Day in the Life of Liz Cross, Training and Staff Services Manager, Merseyside Improved Houses

### Personal Profile

I regard myself as a 'people person', interested in developing and supporting individuals in all areas of life. My interest in the study of people started very early when I took my first course in Transactional Analysis in a Canadian school, at the ripe old age of eleven! Since then, I have continued my formal and informal education in Canada and the UK, and I have undertaken social research in Kenya and Israel.

My first degree is in psychology in which I concentrated on the study of social psychology and the psychology of women. The work I do may be best described as organizational psychology or strategic human resources management. The

111

latter I have developed further by studying for an MSc in business administration. I have worked as a teacher of psychology, a personal development trainer, and management consultant in the public, private and voluntary sectors. All of my work has been carried out in 'political' environments in which my strong commitment to equal opportunities has been an asset. I now work for Merseyside Improved Houses, and manage fourteen staff, who work in personnel, training and catering.

## Organizational Profile

Merseyside Improved Houses is the largest regional provider of voluntary sector housing in Britain. Established in 1928, the association has grown from a small landlord to an organization which owns and manages around 17,000 homes in a wide geographical area. The association employs over 600 full- and part-time staff and has seven regional offices. It calls upon a wide range of skills and enterprise from a dedicated staff, many of whom have worked for the organization for some time. The organization seeks to develop its staff regularly and sets an annual target of ten days' training per full-time member of staff.

## A Typical Day

08.30. *Clarity and Choices.* Drop my staff a line about the recent directors' decision to 'consolidate' job titles. This may result in a change in some of my staff's job titles and I am keen to find out their preferences within the constraints set by the new policy.

08.50. *Confidence, Commitment and Creativity.* Clear out and prioritize my in-tray. Most of the contents can be delegated to others in the team. Delegation is not abdication and we will discuss the outcomes at my monthly individual review meetings with staff. We will both get a chance to hold each other to account. I will measure the effort my staff make to achieve the targets set, and they will get the chance to question whether I was clear in my request and gave them sufficient support or information.

I enjoy these review meetings and I have been delighted by some of the creative solutions that have been developed. If there's a problem, we discuss what happened and how it could be tackled differently next time. During these reviews, I give staff positive, as well as constructive, feedback and thank them for their efforts.

09.25. *Customers and Choices*. Another manager pops in for some professional advice. A member of their staff has said they are pregnant and they are unsure of the law or the terms and conditions of employment regarding this. Provide details of current legislation and policies and outline information on new European directives. We explore the range of choices open to the manager.

10.00. *Creativity*. Go through to see my director. I need some papers signing and feel like a chat about what's on the horizon. I've always got a dozen new 'good' ideas, generated by myself or members of my staff. I enjoy bouncing them off my director to see if there is any mileage to be gained in pursuing some of them with my team.

10.45. *Commitment and Choices*. I have a number of calls to return and some messages from my staff. I try to answer all the queries my staff have first so that they can get on with their work rather than wait for some information from me. One of my staff has been waiting for me to sign a letter to allow her to send it by first-class post. I sign it and promise to raise the issue with my director so she is not left hanging around again for such a minor matter.

11.15. *Commitment and Co-operation*. Finish the report I was working on last night which is to go to the directors' meeting in two weeks' time. The report is based on some project work that three of my staff and I have been working on. All the staff have now given me their information and I want to get it finished today in order to circulate it to them first. Their commitment to making a contribution to this has been invaluable and the work they did in getting other service users in the organization to participate will really pay off when the final report is debated.

12.30. *Clarity and Creativity*. 'Clock off' the flexitime system to have some lunch in the staff restaurant. Clocking off, however, doesn't involve switching off as some of my most important feedback from my internal customers is gathered in the canteen. One of the directors joins me and talks about the employment of temporary staff. I note that I need to ask one of my team to prepare a guidance note on good practice when employing temporary staff.

Spot a colleague from one of our regional offices. She tells me that a change which I had introduced is causing some problems at her office. I listen and agree that we need to explore the issue as a group.

14.00. *Commitment*. The ESF (European Social Fund) bid I've been sweating over for the last week has now been typed and printed. The front page names all those who have helped me put together the information for the bid. I take a copy to each team leader and contributor so they can see what their effort has helped produce.

14.20. *Creativity and Customers*. I have a wander around the office to see what is going on. I have three teams, one of which is located in a different part of the same floor. I go and see how one of them, who had injured their arm, is getting on back at work; have a chat about how best to avoid the same kind of accident again. I will undertake a proper inspection of their work space tomorrow.

14.45. *Co-operation, Commitment and Confidence*. Prepare for my 3 o'clock meeting with the training team. We met four weeks ago to start to design a team development plan. We look at the organization's objectives and strategies for the 1990s, the departmental annual strategy, and the team's annual targets. We consider what part we, as individuals and as a group, have to play in shaping and delivering the strategy. The hardest part of this meeting is to inspire my staff to have confidence in their excellent abilities.

15.00. *Confidence and Clarity*. We meet to consider the report and discuss the action plans for each member of staff. I notice the increase in confidence of a staff member who has already done her action plan.

17.00. *Customers and Choices*. Meet with a colleague who wants to discuss a difficult area of work. We discuss the problem and some tools and techniques that could be used to turn it into an opportunity.

17.45. Time I was gone. I dash from the building hoping I will catch my young son up and ready for a play.

---

**Liz**

- Creates time to bounce around ideas with her manager/colleagues

- Challenges and eliminates unnecessary bureaucracy

- Names the people who help her to prepare any report

- Uses Personal Action Plans to inspire staff to have confidence in their own abilities

- Involves her team in planning for the future

- Gains constant feedback from internal customers

- Informs staff about proposed organizational changes

---

# A Day in the Life of Dr Cheryle Berry, Headteacher, High Storrs School, Sheffield

## *Personal Profile*

I have taught for twenty-two years in a variety of schools and colleges; grammar, secondary modern, comprehensive schools and a community college. My present headship, at High Storrs School, Sheffield, began in January 1989; previously I had been head of the Sir John Gleed Girls' School, Lincolnshire, for five years. I thoroughly enjoy teaching and working with people of all ages. It is a real privilege to be part of the education process of our young people. I believe that education is a 'life-long process' and that we should all continue learning as individuals.

Throughout my teaching career, I have studied in the evenings, weekends and holidays and have a first-class honours degree in mathematics, an MA in Applied Research in Education and a doctorate in Business Administration.

As a manager I believe in the importance of teamwork and participation to achieve the aims of the school. Education is a partnership of staff, students, parents and governors working together and sharing strengths, for everyone's benefit. I delegate responsibilities as widely as possible, participating in many working parties and meetings, although never chairing them. By design, I only chair meetings of the senior management team.

I have tried to make my office welcoming and informal and encourage staff, students and parents to come and see me. Also, to make the whole school atmosphere positive, supportive and stimulating for learning, so that each individual feels that they are well-known and have a part to play in the school's progress. In addition, I teach and try to be part of new initiatives. It is a vital part of 'keeping in touch' with what is happening in the school.

## *Organizational Profile*

High Storrs is an eleven- to eighteen-year-old co-educational comprehensive school of 1,700 students with over 300 in the sixth form and a staff of 106. The school has a long and fine tradition of academic achievement. It is a grade II listed art deco building, which, thanks to the efforts of staff, parents and students, has now been restored to its former glory. The buildings are set in twenty-six acres of land in the south-west of the city and we have easy access to the Peak National Park, where our students rock climb, abseil and canoe.

The school, which is presently the largest in the city, has a budget of approximately £3 million under the Local Management of Schools, administered by the governors and senior staff. The organizational structures reflect the participative and collaborative management style. The students have a schools council, with representatives from each form, to debate issues and, from this year, a small budget to spend on facilities for the school. There is a strong PTA which has educational, fundraising and social events. Many parents are also members of the Environment and Resources Group and give practical help to improve the school.

## A Typical Day

8.00. *Clarity*. Talk to buildings officer (caretaker) about energy conservation and the new hand driers in toilets. Also check through his report to Governors' Finance and General Purposes Committee tonight, on the efficiency of the present cleaning contract.

8.15. *Customers*. Talk to bursar about the IT training needed for clerical staff and she also advises me about the new photocopier for staff.

8.25. *Choices*. Open mail. Talk to deputy who chairs the Curriculum and Staff Development Group about next week's meeting. Arrange to show prospective parent around the school.

8.35. *Confidence*. Child comes to show me athletic award won last night. I am very pleased as she used to be very timid and lacking in confidence.

117

**8.45.** *Commitment*. Talk to deputy in charge of the teachers' appraisal process about the system of pairings for appraisers and appraisees.

**8.55.** *Co-operation*. Daily briefing for all staff. Tell staff that the kitchens have no gas to cook today's lunches (cold food only). Remind staff of social on Friday. Also give reminder of the importance of a consistent policy on homework.

**9.05.** *Creativity*. Assembly with Year 7 in the hall. Congratulate them all on their contributions to last week's Open Day and read them our entry in *The Good State Schools Guide*.

**9.20-10.00.** *Commitment*. Classroom observation of deputy head as part of the appraisal system.

**10.00-10.35.** *Customers*. Walk around the school looking at work. Call in to see how the cook is managing without gas. Call on a drama lesson (promise to come back next week to see how it is progressing).

**10.35-11.00.** *Creativity*. Break in staff room. Congratulate head of music on the concert at the local hospice and the art staff on a design student reaching the last ten of 30,000 entries for the National Award ('Clothes Show Live'); fingers crossed for final.

**11.00-11.40.** *Customers*. Show prospective parents around the school, meeting and talking with staff and students.

**11.40.** *Clarity*. Telephone chair of governors about trip to London to collect the school's Curriculum Award.

**11.50.** *Co-operation*. Telephone head of nearby school to arrange meeting to discuss joint funding bid for TEC money.

**11.55.** *Customers*. Lunch duty. Supervising queues and talking to students in both dining halls. Whilst eating my lunch, talk to deputy about the new LEA funding formula. Patrol around the school, again talking to students and staff.

12.50. *Choices*. Meet group of staff in my room to talk about setting up a new Duke of Edinburgh Bronze Award group.

13.00. *Co-operation*. Telephone call from main office. Child is having severe asthma attack. I contact head of year and parents to arrange transport to children's hospital.

13.10. *Confidence*. Teach Year 10 BTec at City and Guilds Foundation Group. Interactive video, on loan from police, on road safety. Plan visit to local farm next week (health and safety aspects).

14.17. *Commitment*. Talk to group of staff about Lift Appeal social evening. We are trying to raise funds to build a lift to enable our physically handicapped students to have easier access to the first floor.

14.30. *Creativity*. Talk to chair of environment and resources group about a possible painting weekend (for staff, parents and students) to decorate one of the dining halls.

14.45. *Confidence*. Talk to senior teacher in charge of timetable and staffing about our staffing profile projections over the next five years.

15.05. *Commitment*. Meet with senior teacher to discuss national curriculum Key Stage 3 assessment and the Records of Achievement Validation Board.

15.35. *Customers*. Bus duty. Child shows me geography work and asks when am I coming to see their lesson again.

15.50-17.00. *Creativity*. Chair the senior management team meeting. Long-term planning topic national curriculum Key Stage 4.

17.00. *Co-operation*. Telephone call from parent. Child has lost coat. I find coat, telephone back and say the child can collect it from me in the morning.

17.30. *Commitment*. Tour of school looking at corridors, classrooms, toilets, etc. Make notes of items to alert caretaker. Also admire work on display in corridors and classrooms.

17.45. *Customers*. Parent calls on way home from work to discuss child who is ill; we arrange for work to be sent home.

18.10. *Choices*. Telephone call. Parent worried, child not home yet. I telephone friend, discover child is there and had forgotten to tell parents. Telephone parent back to reassure all is all right.

18.30. *Clarity*. Answer letters, fill in forms, put typing in office for secretary, put memos in pigeon holes for relevant staff.

19.15. *Commitment*. Governors' Finance and General Purposes subgroup. Discussion of School Development Plan and budget priorities.

21.30. *Co-operation*. After meeting, talk to chair of governors about next week's Curriculum and Staff Development meeting.

21.50. Leave for home.

22.30. *Confidence, Creativity and Choices*. Arrive home and go out for three-mile jog with my husband. This is my thinking time and a chance to unwind and recharge my mental batteries.

23.30. To sleep (perchance to dream about getting the school lift).

**Cheryle**

- Manages through participation and collaboration
- Delegates the responsibility for chairing the majority of meetings to her staff
- Uses three working groups of staff and governors to plan and implement decisions
- Works co-operatively with another school to gain additional joint funds
- Actively seeks customer feedback each day
- Involves parents and students in creating innovative solutions to problems
- Provides students with the opportunity to debate issues in the school council

# Assessing and Evaluating Your Skills

If we are to survive and thrive in these fast-changing times we need to be constantly gaining feedback on our performance as a manager and be continually developing our skills. There are no longer 'jobs for life' in any organization; our security can be gained from ensuring we have skills and qualifications which are valued in today's and tomorrow's marketplace.

Traditionally managers gain feedback from their line managers through systems of supervision and appraisal; yet their line managers typically are not involved with the details of their work. Many organizations have found that the best people to give managers feedback on their performance as managers are their staff or colleagues who work closely with them. This system is essential when we are focusing on managers supplying a service of management to their staff.

In this chapter we use the Seven Keys to Success as a questionnaire to be completed by you, your staff and relevant colleagues (and by your line manager, if this seems appropriate). For these are the people you are supplying service to, and they can provide constructive feedback on your performance and assist you to target your efforts appropriately and provide continuing customer satisfaction.

This is not a complicated questionnaire and it does not compare you to a standard. The questionnaire assesses two aspects of each practice, i.e., how much you *actually* do this and how much you would *ideally* like to do this in your role, within your organization. Many of the ideas in the Seven Keys to Success may be new to you so this may influence your initial *actual* scores.

The questionnaire has been used by over 200 managers. One colleague who works on his own commented that he found the self-assessment valuable, even though he had no staff to offer the questionnaire to: 'The questionnaire was easy to fill in, quick to do, and immediately highlighted points I hadn't thought about.' Other managers said they received some pleasant surprises; they were not aware that their staff appreciated 'their service' until they received their completed questionnaires.

A number of managers used their feedback as a way to review and change the way they worked with their staff. It provided an appropriate opportunity to introduce more team-working and problem-solving into day-to-day work and also helped to stimulate increased delegation.

## The Seven Keys to Success Questionnaire

Questionnaire 1 should be filled out by you. Questionnaire 1A should be given to your internal customers – your staff and close colleagues with the notes for guidance (p. 128); their answers will help you to assess whether you are providing them with a service of management which meets their needs. If you think it would be helpful, give questionnaire 1A to your manager and ask him/her to assess the service of management you are providing to your internal customers.

## *Completing the questionnaire*

Look at each statement and assess on a scale of 1–10 (1 minimum; 10 maximum).

a) Assess, ideally, how often *I would like to do this* in my work.

Write your assessment in column 1.

b) How much do *I actually do this, in practice*, on a regular basis?

Write your assessment in column 2.

c) Calculate the difference

Take the number in the second column and subtract it from

the number in the first column. Enter your result in the third column.

These results will typically indicate a plus score, i.e., you are doing less of this practice than you would like to. On occasions you may gain a minus score, indicating you are doing more of this practice than you would like to.

d) Record your results

## *An example*

Here is a summary of the scores from a group of eighteen managers who completed the questionnaire.

| Seven Keys | Importance | Actual | Difference |
|---|---|---|---|
| Clarity | 26.6 | 19.9 | 6.7 |
| Customers | 27.9 | 23.0 | 4.9 |
| Confidence | 25.7 | 20.8 | 4.7 (1 reverse) |
| Co-operation | 24.9 | 20.7 | 4.4 (1 reverse) |
| Creativity | 25.0 | 20.5 | 4.9 |
| Commitment | 26.8 | 23.0 | 3.8 |
| Choices | 25.4 | 19.1 | 6.3 |

In two cases, managers had an 'actual' score higher than their 'importance' score, i.e., they felt they were concentrating too much on confidence and co-operation and not achieving a balance of the Seven Keys. These reverse scores distorted and reduced the average differences experienced by others.

# Seven Keys to Success Questionnaire

To be completed by the manager (yourself)

| Statement | Ideal | Actual | Difference |
|---|---|---|---|

Do you, as a manager:

*Clarity*

1. Provide clarity in all your written and verbal communication

2. Show consistency regarding necessary confidentiality

3. Maintain effective systems of information sharing

*Customers*

4. Recognize that you provide a service of management to both internal and external customers

5. Design systems and structures to serve your customers

6. Define quality in terms of customer satisfaction and gain constant customer feedback

*Confidence*

7. Increase the self-confidence of your staff through delegation and providing continual constructive feedback

8. Have the self-confidence to recognize, acknowledge and sort out difficult situations

| Statement | Ideal | Actual | Difference |
|-----------|-------|--------|------------|

9. Seek new ways of doing things, take risks and do things differently

*Co-operation*

10. Agree and work to shared ways of operating with your staff

11. Ensure men and women work together effectively

12. Develop long-term customer—supplier relationships

*Creativity*

13. Use mistakes as learning experiences to improve service

14. Encourage and reward initiative and innovation by your staff

15. Develop your team and gain ideas through shared problem-solving

*Commitment*

16. Value your staff and recognize their different talents

17. Ensure that you and your staff are committed to acting responsibly, hold people accountable for what they do

18. Show commitment to the goals of your team and the purpose of your organization

| Statement | Ideal | Actual | Difference |
|---|---|---|---|

*Choices*

19. Recognize that you can influence all outcomes as you are in control of your response to events

20. Regard issues not as puzzles which have one right answer but as problems which have a range of solutions

21. Transform problems into opportunities

# The Seven Keys to Success Questionnaire 1A

## *Notes for guidance*

This is not a complicated questionnaire and it does not compare your manager to a standard. The questionnaire assesses two aspects of each management practice, i.e., how much your manager *actually* engages in this practice and how much you would *ideally* like him/her to engage in this practice, in the role of manager within your organization. Many of the ideas in the Seven Keys to Success may be new to you so this may influence your initial *actual* scores.

Look at each statement and assess on a scale of 1–10 (1 minimum; 10 maximum).

a) Assess, ideally, how often *I would like my manager to do this* in her/his work.

Write your assessment in column 1

b) How much does *my manager actually do this, in practice*, on a regular basis?

Write your assessment in column 2

c) Calculate the difference

Take the number in the second column and subtract it from the number in the first column. Enter your result in the third column.

These results will typically indicate a plus score, i.e., your manager is doing less of this practice than you would like her/him to do. On occasions you may gain a minus score, indicating your manager is doing more of this practice than you would like her/him to.

d) Return the completed questionnaire to your manager.

ou don't need to write your name on the questionnaire.

e) Provide clarification and comments to your manager

Please give your manager additional comments, explanation and feedback, if you think that these will be helpful to her/him.

# Seven Keys to Success Questionnaire 1A

To be completed by people who receive a service of management from the manager (i.e. staff/colleagues).

**Statement**                                    **Ideal**  **Actual**  **Difference**

Does your manager:

*Clarity*

1. Provide clarity in all her/his written and verbal communication

2. Show consistency regarding necessary confidentiality

3. Maintain effective systems of information sharing

*Customers*

4. Recognize that she/he provides a service of management to both internal customers (i.e., you) and external customers

5. Design systems and structures to serve their customers

6. Define quality in terms of customer satisfaction and gain constant customer feedback

*Confidence*

7. Increase the self-confidence of her/his staff through delegation and providing continual constructive feedback

8. Have the self-confidence to recognize, acknowledge and sort out difficult situations

9. Seek new ways of doing things, take risks and do things differently

### Co-operation

10. Agree and work to shared ways of operating with her/his staff

11. Ensure men and women work together effectively

12. Develop long-term customer–supplier relationships

### Creativity

13. Use mistakes as learning experiences to improve service

14. Encourage and reward initiative and innovation by her/his staff

15. Develop her/his team and gain ideas through shared problem-solving

### Commitment

16. Value her/his staff and recognize their different talents

17. Ensure that she/he and her/his staff are committed to acting responsibly; hold people accountable for what they do

18. Show commitment to the goals of her/his team and the purpose of the organization

*Choices*

19. Recognize that she/he can influence all outcomes as she/he is in control of her/his response to events

20. Regard issues not as puzzles which have one right answer but as problems which have a range of solutions.

21. Transform problems into opportunities

## Recording your results

Write down the results recorded in the 'difference' columns on the table below so you can compare your scores with those of your customers and your manager.

| | Your results: | Your Customers' results: A B C D E F | Your Manager's results: |
| --- | --- | --- | --- |
| | *Difference* | *Difference* | *Difference* |
| 1 | | | |
| 2 | | | |
| 3 | | | |
| 4 | | | |
| 5 | | | |
| 6 | | | |
| 7 | | | |
| 8 | | | |
| 9 | | | |
| 10 | | | |
| 11 | | | |
| 12 | | | |
| 13 | | | |
| 14 | | | |
| 15 | | | |
| 16 | | | |
| 17 | | | |
| 18 | | | |
| 19 | | | |
| 20 | | | |
| 21 | | | |

## Using your feedback to further develop your management skills

Feedback is useful in two ways: it tells you what you are doing right, and highlights areas where you are not currently meeting your customers' needs.

It is important initially to acknowledge those areas of your work where both you and your customers are satisfied. In Tom Peters'[1] terms you need to 'celebrate small wins'. Then, if you are to maximize on the usefulness of the feedback, you need also to make plans to improve your service of management. The more specific you can be in this planning, the easier it becomes to implement your proposals.

Planning change can sometimes be a daunting and lonely task. It involves moving away from the familiar, taking risks, testing out new ideas and checking to see if your new initiatives are successfully meeting the needs of your customers. Think about how you can find people to help you during this process of planning and implementing new ideas. If a group of managers in an organization were using these questionnaires at the same time, for instance, they could provide each other with mutual support. Some line managers may also be keen to help with this process as part of regular supervision. Alternatively some organizations have training co-ordinators who are willing to assist in planning change.

The most important element of planning, though, is to be specific in the goals you set, and to be realistic about the time scales you allocate for each goal.

## Creating goals to further improve your effectiveness as a manager of people

This is a simple goal-setting process which helps you to address the seven most significant areas highlighted in your feedback.

I have suggested starting with the seven most significant differences as this seems a realistic number of changes to tackle at any one time. When you have achieved those seven you may want to repeat this process with other significant differences.

a) Using your results sheet, compare your own scores and those of your customers and manager. Identify the seven highest or most significant scores and start with these. One manager commented:

> *If my results and those of my seven staff all indicate a large difference on point 1, then I am getting a powerful message about improving my communication skills.*

b) Think about how you might be able to improve your performance in these seven areas.

c) Create goals for change, highlighting the first three action steps, and give each goal a date by which you aim to achieve that goal, identifying when you need to monitor your progress (columns 1–3).

## Improving your skills

**Goals and Action Steps**               **Start   Monitor   Finish**

First Goal

Initial Action Steps
a)
b)
c)

Second Goal

Initial Action Steps
a)
b)
c)

Third Goal

Initial Action Steps
a)
b)
c)

**Fourth Goal**

**Initial Action Steps**
a)
b)
c)

**Fifth Goal**

**Initial Action Steps**
a)
b)
c)

**Sixth Goal**

**Initial Action Steps**
a)
b)
c)

**Seventh Goal**

**Initial Action Steps**
a)
b)
c)

## Reassessing Your Performance

When you consider that you have achieved your goals it may be helpful to get your internal customers to complete questionnaire 1A again so that you can assess the change in your scores since your initial assessment.

### *Living My Writing*

When I was part way through writing this book, Steve Rick of the Royal Bank of Scotland reminded me that the challenge for me was not only to finish the book but constantly to use the principles in my day-to-day work and to 'live my writing'.

I have recently completed questionnaire 1, and my secretary and a colleague I work closely with have completed questionnaire 1A. I used this feedback to create my own action plan which I am now in the process of implementing. I plan to ask them to complete questionnaire 1A in six months' time to assess my improvements.

# Conclusion

John Bennington, director of the local government centre, Warwick University, was a guest speaker at the Waves of Change conference at Sheffield Hallam University in 1993. In reply to a question from the floor about who he thought would be the leaders of tomorrow, he stressed that he didn't think it was a question of the leaders, but rather of leadership. He said that everyone contributes to the leadership process, so we are all the leaders of tomorrow.

In the same way, new managers are not led; they lead. This leadership is not the traditional leadership of the past, when heroes responded to crises, but a new interpretation of leadership which encompasses proactivity, enabling and flexibility. Peter Senge comments:[1]

> *The new view of leadership in learning organizations centres on subtler and more important tasks. In a learning organization, leaders are designers, stewards and teachers. They are responsible for* building organizations *where people continually expand their capabilities to understand complexity, clarify vision, and improve shared mental models – that is, they are responsible for learning.*

Learning to manage people is a continuous process, which never stops. In the flatter organizations of the future, managers will need vision, values and an ability to constantly re-evaluate their work to enable them to provide a service of management which continually delights their customers.

# Summary of the Models

Photocopy these summaries and put them on your wall

## Positive Assumptions for Managing People

1. Managing people is about **managing our relationships with other people**

   Event + Response leads to Outcome

   We are in charge of our responses

2. Individuals can do anything they want to – **if it interests them**. If they don't know how to do it they can learn

3. **Everyone has potential** – in some people it is hidden and has to be identified by others

4. Everyone is **responsible** for what he/she does and can be held **accountable** for what he/she does, providing he/she has been given appropriate authority

5. Often we have to **let go of old habits** before we can adopt new ways of doing things

6. **Everyone has his/her own view of the world** and that can never be exactly the same as another person's, for he/she has not shared the same life experience

7. **Everything** and **everyone** is constantly changing

Vivien Whitaker, *Managing People*, HarperCollins, 1994

# Seven Keys to Success

1 . Clarity
- provide clarity in all your written and verbal communication
- show consistency regarding necessary confidentiality
- maintain effective systems of information-sharing

2 . Customers
- recognize that you provide a service of management to both internal and external customers
- design systems and structures to serve your customers/patients/students
- define quality in terms of customer satisfaction and gain constant customer feedback

3 . Confidence
- increase the self-confidence of your staff through delegation and providing continual constructive feedback
- have the self-confidence to recognize, acknowledge and sort out difficult situations
- seek new ways of doing things, take risks and do things differently

4 . Co-operation
- agree and work to shared ways of operating with your staff
- ensure men and women work together effectively
- develop long-term customer–supplier relationships

5 . Creativity
- use mistakes as learning experiences to improve service
- encourage and reward initiative and innovation by your staff
- develop your team and gain ideas through shared problem-solving

6 . Commitment
- value your staff and recognize their different talents

- ensure that you and your staff are committed to acting responsibly. Hold people accountable for what they do
- show commitment to the goals of your team and the purpose of your organization

## 7. Choices

- recognize that you can influence outcomes as you are in control of your response to events
- regard issues not as puzzles which have one right answer but as problems which have a range of solutions
- transform problems into opportunities

Vivien Whitaker, *Managing People*, HarperCollins, 1994

# Further Reading

## Cheap, cheerful and easy to read:

CLUTTERBUCK, D: *Everyone Needs a Mentor*, IPM 2nd edition, 1992

CLUTTERBUCK, D and SNOW, D: *Working with the Community – A Guide to Corporate Social Responsibility*, Weidenfeld Paperbacks, 1990

GARRATT, R: *Learning to Lead*, Successful Manager Series, HarperCollins, 1991

GLOUBERMAN, D: *Life Choices and Life Changes Through Imagework – The Art of Developing Personal Vision*, Unwin Paperbacks, 1989

HOLLAND, S and WARD, C: *Assertiveness: A Practical Approach*, Winslow Press, 1990

HOPSON, B and SCALLY, M: *Communication: Time to Talk*, Mercury Business Paperbacks, 1992

HOPSON, B, SCALLY, M and STAFFORD, K: *Transitions: The Challenge of Change*, Mercury Business Paperbacks, 1992

HUGHES, J M: *Counselling for Managers – An Introductory Guide*, Bacie, 1991

LARSON, C and LA FASTO, F: *Teamwork – What Must Go Right, What Can Go Wrong*, Sage Publications, 1989

POSTLE, D: *The Mind Gymnasium – A New Age Guide to Personal Growth*, Papermac, 1988

## Longer, more expensive, but worth the investment:

PEDLER, M, BURGOGNE, J, and BOYDELL, T: *The Learning Company*, McGraw Hill, 1991

STEINEM, G: *Revolution From Within: A Book of Self-Esteem*, Bloomsbury, 1992

MEGGINSON, D and PEDLER, M: *Self Development: A Facilitator's Guide*, McGraw Hill, 1992

# Resources

## Support

Join the Association for Management, Education and Development (AMED) and use their Regional Network to discover like-minded people.

AMED
21 Catherine Street
London
WC2B 5JS
Tel: 071 497 3264

Institute of Management
Management House
Cottingham Road
Corby
N17 1TT

Institute of Training and Development
Marlow House
Institute Road
Marlow
SL7 1BD

## Information

Local Business Library

Tapes and videos – Careertrack, Milton Keynes, UK

Local Chamber of Commerce/local TEC

## Courses

Qualification courses: seek information from your local universities and colleges for full- or part-time courses, including day-release

## An invitation to send in examples of good practice:

I am keen to hear about other examples of good practice in managing people. If you have an example that you would like to share please send the details to:

Vivien Whitaker
16 Rutland Terrace
Barlow
Sheffield
S18 5SS
Telephone & Fax: 0742 891367

Thank you for sharing your experience.

# Notes

## Chapter 1

1. Charles Handy, *The Age of Unreason*, Arrow, 1990
2. Brian Dumaine, 'The New Non-Manager Managers', *Fortune Magazine*, 22 February 1993
3. Rosemary Stewart, *Managing Today and Tomorrow*, Macmillan, 1991
4. Diane Summers, 'Managers find block on career progress', *Financial Times*, 17 May 1993
5. Chris Lorenz, 'Rambo Bosses Back Off', *Financial Times*, 18 September 1992

## Chapter 4

1. Edgar Schein, *Process Consultation*, Addison Wesley, 1969
2. Jack Canfield, *Self Esteem and Peak Performance*, Careertrack Tapes (Milton Keynes)
3. Mark Brown, 'How to Create Success', *Management Today Journal*, January 1984
4. Jack Canfield, op. cit.
5. Dina Glouberman, *Life Choices and Life Changes Through Imagework, The Art of Developing Personal Vision*, Unwin Paperbacks, 1989
6. James Brian Quinn, Henry Mintzberg, Robert M. James, *The Strategy Process – Concepts, Contexts and Cases*, Prentice Hall International, 1988

## Chapter 5

1. Peter Drucker, *Harvard Business Review*, Winter, 1988
2. Obtainable from AMED: 21 Catherine Street, London WC2B 5JS
3. John A. Carlisle and Robert C. Parker, *Beyond Negotiation: Redeeming Customer-Supplier Relationships*, John Wiley & Sons Ltd, reprinted January 1990
4. Gareth Morgan, *Images of Organization*, Sage, 1986

5. John Michael Hughes, *Counselling for Managers – An Introductory Guide*, Bacie, 1991
6. David Clutterbuck, *How to Be a Good Corporate Citizen: A Manager's Guide to Making Social Responsibility Work – and Pay*, McGraw-Hill, 1981
7. ibid.
8. John Griffiths, 'Driven Towards Leanness', *Financial Times*, 10 March 1993
9. Michael Hammer, 'Re-engineering Work: Don't Automate, Obliterate', *Harvard Business Review*, July–August 1990
10. Adrian Furnham, 'When Employees Rate Their Superiors', *Financial Times*, 1 March 1993
11. Gloria Steinem, *Revolution from Within – A Book of Self-Esteem*, Bloomsbury Publishing, 1992
12. Mary Lou Leavitt, *Conflict Resolution*, Quaker pamphlet
13. Jack Canfield, *Self-Esteem and Peak Performance*, Careertrack Tapes
14. Susan Jeffers, *Dare to Connect – How to Create Confidence, Trust and Loving Relationships*, Piatkus Books, 1992
15. ibid.
16. Nicole Dickenson, 'Catering for the ethical shopper', *Financial Times*, 15 April 1993
17. Gareth Morgan, *Creative Organization Theory*, Sage, 1989
18. Nicole Dickenson, op.cit.
19. Dick Lohr, *How to Delegate Work*, Careertrack Tapes

## Chapter 7

1. Tom Peters, *Thriving On Chaos*, Macmillan London Ltd, 1988

## Conclusion

1. Peter M. Senge, *The Fifth Discipline*, Century Business, 1990

# Index